HOW TO STOP WORRYING

GUIDE TO END WORRIES & OVERCOME ANXIETY, STOP PANIC ATTACKS, ELIMINATE NEGATIVE THINKING AND START LIVING YOUR BEST LIFE NOW.

By Roberta Rivera

Table of Contents

Introduction

The first thing that we must face in our quest to learn to think positively is that most of us often think in a very negative manner. Why do we think so negatively? Well, it's a very complex answer and so it must be broken down into several large chunks.

For the most part, our negative thought patterns stem from experiences, things that have shaped us in such a way that cause us to think negative things. These negative experiences, especially at a young age, teach us what we believe to be truths and as such, we live out of these truths.

Consider for a moment, how we learn as children. When we look up at the sky and see a bird, we will point at it and say "bird!" Our parents say "yes, you're right!" Then we see an airplane fly by and we point again and yell out "bird!" Our parents correct us this time and say "no, that's an airplane." Up until the moment that new information is introduced to us, we will operate off of the things that we have already learned to be true. As we grow up, we start to have experiences which cause us to form a belief. Until we are corrected by an outside source, we will believe most negative experiences as true. Imagine if that child's parents had not bothered to correct him, or most likely his parents simply weren't there to correct him when he saw the airplane. He would live the rest of his life believing that airplanes are birds until someone corrects him.

The problem with negative thinking is that we often don't have anyone help us in correcting it because it's much harder to see than a simple error like mistaking a bird for a plane. Cynicism, black and white thinking, catastrophizing, polarization and other negative thought patterns are often mistook for as personality traits and we adapt to them. In some cases, such as being overly cynical, we can become proud of these negative thought patterns. They become a part of our identity and as such, we find that they become integral to who we are.

So the first thing to know about why negative thoughts are within in us is that they are bred by experiences. Either someone told us something that hurt us, something happened that caused us to believe a certain truth or we came to something on our own conclusion without anyone telling us otherwise. As these untruths and negatives took hold in our minds, they grew stronger and became more a part of our personalities. Eventually, we started to recognize them as a part of ourselves and so we don't seek to change these negativities because to us they are a way of life now.

This might seem absurd to an outsider, of course. The idea that we keep negative thought processes willingly might seem like a person is willfully hurting themselves, but the truth is they don't know any other way until corrected! Just like the little boy who has no idea that gigantic mechanical jet isn't a bird, so do those of us who have a negative outlook on life fail to realize that we are suffering. Many times we don't even notice it because we have grown so used to the way we think.

What about you? Do you think that maybe you have some negative thought patterns that you are living out but haven't really spent a lot of time thinking about them? It's normal for everyone to have some degree of negative thinking, so let's go ahead and take a look at a few major examples of what's known as a cognitive distortion. A cognitive distortion is essentially a pattern of thinking that has very specific traits. Read through the list and see if you fit any of these categories:

Black and White Thinking:

Black and white thinking, also known as polarization, is a kind of thought pattern where you judge things as either good or bad. This is taken to an extreme in a black and white thinker, however, and they don't simply look at things as shades of gray, rather everything has to be good or bad. They are quick to make judgments about a situation, seeing a positive thing as good or looking at a negative thing as bad. There's no wiggle room with a black and white thinker. If a project has imperfections, it is a "failure." If they are happy with something they are "ecstatic." The extremes are intense with a polarized thinker and they often live out of these extremes. Tension can rise when they begin sorting people into the good or bad category and oftentimes they will find themselves dealing with themselves and others harshly.

Catastrophizing:

Catastrophizing is the act of thinking about something and taking it to the most dangerous and illogical conclusion. For example, if someone is on an airplane and they hear a bumping sound, if they were a catastrophizer they would quickly come to think that the plane was going to crash, going immediately to the worst case scenario as opposed to trying to figure out what made that noise. In relationships a catastrophizer might become obsessive, worried when their friends don't text them back that their friend is either dead or now hates them. Someone who has a catastrophic thought pattern often finds themselves constantly in a state of worry or anxiety.

Emotional Reasoning:

Emotional reasoning is where a person tends to allow their feeling to influence what they believe to be true instead of looking at the reality of the situation. For example, if a person feels that they are ugly, they will believe they are ugly, regardless of what others around them tell them. An emotional truth creates the specific reality for said individual and they live in a constant state of intense, emotional pain because of this false reality.

Filtering:

There are usually positives and negatives to most situations. Life is rarely one dimension and as such, there are good things and bad things in just about any situation. A person who has a filtering type of thought pattern will zero in on the bad, focusing primarily on the things that are negative in the situation as opposed to looking at the big picture and seeing the truth for what it is. Filtering often makes a bad situation worse and negates the chance for any kind of good thing to be seen in positive situations.

Personalization:

Personalization is where an individual sees themselves as primarily to blame for everything that happens around them, regardless of whether they had a direct hand in it or not. If someone with that personalization thought pattern were to see a car accident that was nearby them, they might think that they were somehow responsible for it. If some kind of tragedy befell a friend, they might feel they have something to with the situation, even if they did not.

Over-generalization:

When a person over-generalizes, they are reacting to a very small specific amount of information and then they apply it to an entire situation. For example, if it rains once on the way to a picnic, the over-generalizer will say "it always rains on a picnic." They think in always and never statements. In their relationships they might say "you always talk about yourself' or "you never pay attention to me." In their minds they might feel that the situation always happens one way or another due to experiences. This can lead them to believe something different from reality and reacting differently than other people would. How would you react as if every single time you went on a picnic, it rained? Regardless of the reality, the over-generalizer reacts that way each time, even if it only happened once.

Mind Reading:

Someone who has the negative thought patterns of mind reading might find themselves trying to guess what other people are thinking. This mind reading often believes that others are thinking negatively or that their intentions are meant to cause them harm. Mind reading is a way for a person to jump to conclusions, inferring what they believe about someone without having sufficient evidence. Thinking "no one has texted me all week, they must hate me," is an example of mind reading. The only piece of information this individual has is that they haven't been texted and with that information they are able to jump to the conclusion that they are disliked.

Giving Up Control:

Some individuals believe that they honestly do not have any control in their life. Things are always someone else's fault. They struggle to take responsibility because they honestly believe that other factors are always responsible for their behavior. "I'm sorry I was angry with you but I was hungry" is a statement that gives up control for an active choice. Instead, they are choosing to blame some other source for what happened. This can also apply to accuse people of making us feel certain emotions. When a person transfers responsibility to someone or something else, they are adopting a thought pattern of refusing to change themselves.

Splitting:

Splitting is the attitude of all or nothing. Either a person is willing to keep their room absolutely spotless or it will be an absolute cesspool of filth. Either they are going to work out every single day or they will not work out at all. This all or nothing attitude infiltrates just about every facet of an individual's life. It can cause immense strain on their relationships, friendships and choices in life. The idea that things have to be perfect or they are terrible will essentially create a false belief that things are either much better or much worse than they really are.

When we look at all of these negative thought patterns, it's no wonder that the world is in such a state! The seeds of these various different patterns work to sabotage us as we begin to try and adapt to new patterns. The brain is very interested in confirming what it knows to be true. Once we adopt a negative thought pattern, our minds become very protective of these thought patterns and as such they grow to become a part of us.

So why do we develop such patterns of thought? Do negative experiences really have the ability to affect how we look at life? The answer is a resounding yes! All of the negative things that you experience in your life, especially at the early stages, have a lot to do with how we begin to develop these negative patterns of thought.

HY WE WORRY

When we worry about something that has not yet happened, we focus all our energy on anticipating something that might never happen. In this way, we occupy our mind with negative thoughts that have no other result than to attract other negativity.

When we are worried, we do not fully live the present and, furthermore, we cloud the experiences we are experiencing due to our pessimistic vision. In fact, most of our concerns have to do with something we have no control over. We can, therefore, worry as much as we want, but this will not solve the problem in any way, indeed: most of the time, what we are so concerned with will not turn out to be as terrible as we imagined.

Excessive worry easily turns into anxiety, fear of what we do not know and of the future. In this way, worries affect both our physical and emotional health, leading to stress and anxiety disorders. When we live constantly worried, our body is in a state of continuous alert, as if it were always in danger; this condition, on the other hand, should only occur sometimes and not often.

Little by little, therefore, we lose the ability to evaluate situations objectively, and we take for granted that life hides many dangers; in this way, we preclude the possibility of relaxing and enjoying beautiful things. We live every situation as a conflict or something to resolve, even when it comes to insignificant commitments.

The concerns are both unnecessary and harmful. This evidence known to most people does not always protect us from the anxiety we feel about something that is about to happen. Near an important date, it sometimes happens to be struck by an irrational fear that leads to making rash choices, to assume a suspicious and hypercritical attitude, to conceive of little objective and defeatist thoughts. What brain mechanisms regulate this complex function? What role does the individual will play in the management of this psychic experience?

According to the research conducted by Dr. Joseph LeDoux at the University of New York, the repercussions of the aforementioned mental ruminations on the well-being experienced would be very strong since the reaction generated by a situation that causes apprehension is hardly composed and balanced. In fact, we tend to exaggerate when we find ourselves thinking about what awaits us self-inflicting us with weary psychological suffering.

However, science provides us with an excuse for not attributing total responsibility for the illness to the person's will. The amygdala treats and evaluates incoming stimuli responding to a possible danger with the release of some neurotransmitters, such as dopamine, capable of producing a generalized alert state. The information is then transmitted to the encephalic cortex, which processes the received information in a logical and rational manner.

Emotions are, therefore, as reiterated by LeDoux, generated before thought. The latter often fails to impose itself on the affective flux already triggered leaving us at the mercy of our troubles. Hyper stimulation of the amygdala then causes reduced functioning of the cerebral cortex and hyperactivity of the anterior cingulate cortex where the pain is located.

The suffering that we perceive in such situations is revealed, therefore, real and responsive to precise encephalic mechanisms. Furthermore, if the aforementioned condition persists, we may encounter cognitive, attentive, and decision-making problems. Such widespread impairment of intellectual faculties will not only affect the quality of the behaviors acted out, but also the lucidity and objectivity experienced by the subject.

Knowing how to manage what we feel is not at all easy. Sometimes the approach of an event that is very important to us cannot leave us indifferent. However, it is necessary to recognize the value we attribute to it and the apprehension that it gives us, because of the success of the activity we care so much about. Only by openly facing our experiences can we not remain a victim and bring home the desired result.

I don't know people who have never worried about something in their lives. Whether it's a job interview, a question at school, a plane trip, a health problem, or something more trivial, we all had a moment of anxiety.

These moments are not pleasant, we know, because when we are worried, we are emotionally paralyzed, we isolate ourselves from the rest of the world and remain focused exclusively on the situation that concerns us. This becomes our unique and pounding thought for whole days and prevents us from serenely carrying out our activities, which is why it is fundamental to learn to stop worrying excessively about something before this state of mind turns into a real pathology

If you are a person who cares what I would like to tell you is that you are not alone. We all worry less intensely. Worry is a "thought that occupies our mind" generating anxiety, restlessness, tension, problems in sleep. Let's try together to understand what it is.

The concern is the main component of all anxiety and depression disorders. For this reason, it seems appropriate to observe this phenomenon to prevent and promote our psychological health.

There are different types of concerns; each of us can experience one or more of these in our lives (Leahy 2005):

being rejected

being alone

making an exam wrong

not looking pleasant

what other people think of us

getting sick

falling from a height

having a plane crash

losing your money

being late

going crazy

having thoughts and strange sensations

to be humiliated

The concerns are, therefore accompanied by thoughts on the concerns themselves. We can often tell ourselves that "we know that we are expecting the worst, but we cannot fail to do it" or "even if people tell me that all is well I cannot stop worrying."

We, therefore, come to believe that we cannot control our thoughts and that this could be a problem for our mental health.

Where It Originates From

According to the researches, having experimented in their environment of growth, life history and learning about traumas linked to the threat of their physical health can contribute to the onset of experiences of concern (of various kinds) in adulthood. The significant family models characterized by concern and hyper-protection often provide conditioning and reinforcement of the use of these strategies (the outside world is dangerous).

In these environments of growth, there seems to be difficulty in the expression of emotions and in providing a warm and safe environment. In some cases, children find themselves parents of their parents. A loss of the parent before the age of 16 and in general, a type of attachment with insecure family members they produce a living environment that is perceived as risky and a source of alarm.

Even shame is a very significant issue in keeping the trend worry. In a situation whereby we hear " what they think of you? " The message we receive is that what we are or do must be hidden and not shared, because it would not be accepted.

Because we worry

The reason we use concern is that this strategy seems to make sense to us.

We can believe that in this way we will find a solution. In some cases, it may seem that worrying allows us not to forget things. Generally, the worry is intended to anticipate and may diminish the feeling of getting unprepared for events.

A rather interesting thing is the socially acceptable meaning that can convey the concern: if I worry it means that I am a responsible person and this will make me appreciable by others.

People don't want to worry. It is certainly not their main purpose. The concern is a means of facing situations that we consider dangerous, uncertain, out of control.

The reason why we worry is that we believe we must do it:

we believe that concern helps us solve problems

we believe that the world is dangerous and that we do not have the resources to face it

we believe that concern helps us to avoid thinking about the worst possible consequences of an event

we believe that worry keeps us safe from too strong emotions

we believe that concern contains our anxiety

we believe we have control

we believe we are more responsible

we believe we are reducing uncertainties

we believe we control thoughts and emotions

we believe we have more motivation

But does all this work?

Our mind is not used to falsify. This means that we are inclined to use the knowledge we have learned and not to question it so easily. All this has an "economic" meaning. We save energy. But it can be a fallacious strategy. In some cases, it is necessary to collect information to verify or falsify our ideas.

"If I am certain that riding a bicycle is dangerous, I will never try to give it a try. The worry is so strong that I cannot allow myself to experiment."

In this case, we can immediately observe how concern, rather than motivating our intentionality, tends to limit it and lead us to procrastinate important things.

In short, the concern seems to produce problems instead of diminishing them.

Some thoughts on this:

I am sure that all this will seem familiar to those who have experienced the concern. Surely you have done your best to try to counter it. But it didn't always work. Sometimes what seems to help us is instead something that keeps the problem itself.

Chapter 1 Stop Worrying

There are some things in life that you cannot control. Unfortunately, not everyone can accept the hard truth of that reality. They either can't accept it, or they won't. Those who resist and right against the truth are usually the ones who tend to be control freaks. They try to micromanage, attempt to force others to go along with what they want, and they're reluctant to delegate tasks. They believe that controlling everything is the only way to stop "bad things" they are so worried about from happening, and when they realize they can't force the outcome that they want, they become anxious.

No one wants to deal with the unpleasant moments in life. If we could, we'd only want to fill our lives with nothing but happy memories and fun times and fast forward over the unpleasant bits. If only it worked that way. For most people, this doesn't bother them as much. They accept that sometimes in life, not everything will go your way and that's okay. They pick themselves up and move on. For chronic worries, however, they may know that worrying about disasters is not going to change anything, but they choose to do it anyway. They can't help themselves. They spend all that time consumed by their worries they let other responsibilities they should be focusing on get neglected. At the end of the day, they might realize their worrying did them no good, but they'll repeat the cycle again tomorrow. That's the only way they know how to cope with the stress that comes their way.

Everyone has a unique way of reacting to stress. Some can remain cool and calm under pressure, while others let themselves get swept away in the sea of their emotions. Stress impacts us in different ways, and to overcome your worries, you need to identify what your triggers are and the way that you respond when you feel pressured. Once you've identified the pattern of behavior that emerges each time you're stressed, you can work on making the necessary adjustments and develop more effective coping strategies that will strengthen you instead of breaking you down. Stress and worries can be a fuel for positive change, but only if you learn to control your emotions.

Morphing from Stress to Worries and Anxieties

Most people would react to stress by trying to push it away, avoid it, or suppress it. It's not an emotion they want to deal with. That's understandable. In large quantities, stress can do all sorts of things to your body.

But why does stress happen? Is it always bad? Not necessarily. Imagine yourself standing in the middle. On one side, you've got demand, and on the other, capacity. You're right in the middle of the two. The stress you feel is based on your capacity to meet demand, bridging the gap between the two. Stress is neither good nor bad. Instead, it is the way you use it that makes the difference.

The energy of stress that is felt when trying to bridge the gap between demand and capacity. When the energy overwhelms you, that's when stress turns negative. Some people are able to turn this energy into the fuel that they need to channel their focus and aligning their priorities to meet the necessary demand. When that happens, the energy of stress becomes positive. It all comes down to you and how you respond when you're faced with your stress triggers.

Stress starts off as energy, but it can quickly morph into worries the moment you allow yourself to get swallowed up by the emotions that you feel. That can steadily grow worse when your worries get bigger and bigger. Instead of feeling stressed about one problem, your mind drifts towards other issues that are not related to the present problem you face. Maybe you start worrying about what you should have done, or what you could have done, or wished you had done better on problems that are not directly related to what you're having to face right now. All your thoughts start to run together, getting jumbled up until you're not sure what you're worried about anymore. All you know is that you're feeling anxious and finding it difficult to relax.

Our ability to worry is the brain's way of protecting us from the possibilities we might have to encounter, which can be a good thing if we approach from a problem-solution perspective. When you're stuck on your worries and unable to move forward, though, it becomes a problem. That's when worries began to shift towards the anxiety spectrum as it starts to intensify. Worry is more of a mental construct whereas anxiety lingers in your body. Anxiety heightens your nervous system and when you get stuck in this state for a prolonged period, your inability to relax and calm the body down is going to be a disadvantage. Anxiety causes a lot of your body's systems to go into overdrive from the hormones that are being churned out. Your heart rate escalates, you have trouble breathing, there's a tightness in your chest, or you're shaking and trembling. We're not meant to experience these sensations for long, and when your body doesn't get the time it needs to recover and truth to normal, it's going to affect your health and wellbeing in the long run.

Despite it all, we need stress, anxiety, and worries in our life to a certain extent. There's a reason we're hardwired for these emotions. They serve a purpose. They give us the information we need to react in ways that ensure our survival and safety. Trying to ignore them or suppress them doesn't make them go away. They'll be there, bubbling beneath the surface, causing a serious imbalance in our mental and emotional state. Like a volcano that is waiting to erupt, all those pent up emotions will burst forth at once and it won't be pretty. However, if we learned to identify our triggers, emotions, and behavior and used it to our advantage instead, we could mobilize the stressful energy. In doing so, we effectively using this energy as fuel instead of a reason to break us down.

Who Are the Ones Who Worry?

Besides the perfectionists and control freaks, there is another personality type who is also susceptible to worries. These are the people who carry the "What if" syndrome with. These individuals are easily identifiable because they tend to worry about all sorts of things, even when there is no reason to worry. They walk around asking "What if" all the time, and create reasons to worry when reasons don't exist yet. Robert L. Leahy, author of The Worry Cure: 7 Steps to Stop Worry from Stopping You believes this has something to do with genetics and nurture versus non-nurture factors. Those who come from divorced families, for example, have a higher tendency by as much as 70% of developing Generalized Anxiety Disorder (GAD). Overprotective parents tend to raise children who worry too much too.

Worry could be a result of biological and environmental components too. Growing up in an environment with a lot of stress-related triggers, like watching the way your family members cope with their anxiety issues will have some influence over you if that is all you grew up around. It will be the only way you know how to cope with your anxieties too.

What Makes Us Do It?

That's the big question, isn't it? We know worrying does no good, yet we do it anyway and most of us have a hard time explaining why. For the most part, a lot of worriers react the way they do because they believe something bad could or will happen. Therefore, they let themselves believe that if they worry, they might be able to stop the bad thing from happening. To others, it might not make sense, but the mind of the worrier thinks if you can imagine that something bad is going to happen or will happen, you need to worry about it. They see it as a responsibility, almost.

With all the negativity and poor side effects associated with too much worry, it's hard for anyone to remember that worry can sometimes be a good thing. Despite its poor reputation, worry is still first and foremost, our basic survival mechanism. If you could learn to keep your worries under control, it wouldn't be such a bad thing anymore. But when your worries are disproportionate and affect you so deeply it's disrupting your ability to function, then something needs to be done about it and fast!

Reasons You Need to Quit Your Worry

If you wanted to, there will always be a reason to worry. Always. The worries will never end unless you put a stop to it. If you can visualize positive images and scenarios in your mind, like what it feels like to achieve success or see yourself accomplishing your goal, you can certainly control what triggers your worry too. What you're probably lacking right now is the motivation. You need an incentive as to why you should stop, and here are a few reasons to consider:

·   You Won't Change the Outcome - You need to repeat this fact to yourself as many times as needed until the message finally sinks in. you can't change the outcome with worry. Action is what changes the outcome. Solutions change the outcome. Proactiveness changes the outcome. Worry does not.

·   You're Missing Out On A Lot - If there's one important life lesson you need to take away from all this, it is that you're missing out on a lot when you worry. Once a moment is gone, it can never return. What's happening in your present are the treasured moments you need to be focused on. Instead of worrying about what's happened or what is yet to happen, focus on what is happening around you now. Be present and enjoy it as it is because you might regret it later if you don't. If you're busy worrying about what's going to happen next week while your child is learning to take his first steps, you're missing out on one of the most precious moments in your life as a parent and you know that's not what you want to do.

·   Life Is Short - We don't spend nearly enough time reflecting on this. If you knew you were going to die tomorrow, what would you differently today? Would you worry less and seize the moment? You only get one life, and each moment is precious because once it's gone, it is never coming back again. Time doesn't move backward, and it certainly waits for no man. Worriers are missing out on the best part of life, which is a tremendous shame. All worriers tend to do is visualize all the things that could go wrong, fretting about things that they can't control, and completely missing out on the moments happening right in front of them. When you only get one moment to live, is it worth it spending that time unhappy and miserable?

· 	You're Imagining the Worse - Think about all the times you have spent ages worrying about the worst, most disastrous outcome you could think of. How many times did those scenarios manifest? Probably barely or never. How many times has a problem seemed so monumental to you, but when that situation or circumstance actually happens, you find that it wasn't so bad after all? Too many to count? That's what chronic and obsessive worrying will do to you. Worries exaggerate the problems in their heads, making it seem even bigger than it really is. As a result, they tend to overstress and focus on the negatives outcomes of a situation, when there is no real or concrete evidence that it will happen. Our worries are magnified by our imagination, and unless you've got absolute proof that the worst will happen, there's no point letting your imagination carry you away.

·   You're Not Being Constructive - Fretting and predicting the possible problems of the future is not productive, generating solutions to fix those problems or prevent them, is construction. Problem-solving is good, worrying is not. Time to change that pattern of behavior.

·   You'll Find It Hard to Decide Anything - When you worry all the time, it becomes hard for you to make a decision. Each decision seems like it would come with its own set of problems and possible negative outcomes, which causes worriers to worry even more. When they finally do end up making a decision, it may not necessarily be the right decision because their judgment has been clouded by worry.

·   You Can't See the Bright Side of Life - Losing the ability to see the positive side of situations will increase a worrier's levels of anxiety and fear, and do nothing to help quell the overwhelming sense of worry that they feel. When chronic worrying becomes a habit, the worrier loses all ability to see the silver lining in any situation. All they can think about and focus on are the negatives and they look at life as a glass half empty environment. Eventually, it becomes almost impossible to view things positively, even when there is nothing bad to think about.

Stop Worrying About What You Can't Control

You'll be a lot happier and less stressed when you do. If you channeled that time and energy you spent worrying and used it for something more productive instead, think about what a difference it would make in your life. It's going to be a struggle in the beginning, but putting a stop to your worries is not impossible. You need the right push and the right strategies to do it:

·   Identify What Is Within Your Control - Make the first switch by training your mind to focus on identifying what you can control instead. What you've been doing all this time is worrying about what was outside your control. What you're going to do now is repeatedly tell yourself what can I control in this situation? A simple shift in your perspective and you begin to see everything in a different light. You may not be able to stop the bad things from happening, but you can prepare for it by determining which factors you can control. Your reaction is one thing you can control, so start with that and work from there.

·   Think About Your Influence - How much influence do you have on the people who may be involved in the situation you're worried about? You may not be able to force your desired outcome, but what you can do is try to influence or persuade others to see things from your perspective. If everyone is in agreement, you can then work together towards a viable solution. You could be the role model that sets things in motion while everyone else follows your lead. This way, at least you don't have to worry that you're all alone in this.

· No More Feeling Sorry for Yourself - It's the kind of thinking that is going to get you nowhere. Feeling sorry for yourself is self-destructive, and you don't need this habit in your life if you're serious about overcoming your worries and anxiety. When you spend too much time pitying yourself, you don't have time to live it to the fullest. Trade-in self-pity with an attitude of gratitude and watch your worries begin to melt away.

· Identify What You're Afraid Of - In any situation, ask yourself what you're afraid of the most. What would be your worst nightmare come to life in that situation? Are your predictions real and based on facts? Or is your catastrophic outcome based on assumption? Pinpointing your fears makes it easier to see if they are responsible for magnifying the emotions you feel. If your fears feel like they are something that's too much for you to manage alone, it is okay to admit that you might need help or support getting yourself through it. Make a list of your worries, identify each one of them and toss out the ones which are not viable.

· Learn to Differentiate Problem-Solving and Rumination - Problem-solving is always going to be the better approach to take. Ruminating and replaying past scenarios or conversations in your head as you imagine your disastrous outcomes repeatedly is never going to work. What you need to do now is identify how productive the thinking you're engaged in is. How do you find ways to minimize the impact of what you're worried about? As soon as you catch yourself ruminating and not coming up with a solution, switch channels in your brain and go back to problem-solving mode.

· Have A Stress Plan - Get enough sleep. Eat right. Exercise. Do activities that make you happy. Take a day off to pamper yourself. In a nutshell, finding ways to make yourself feel good or happy is your stress plan. You need a way to relieve yourself, everyone does. Whenever you're feeling overwhelmed, it's not wrong to take a break and admit you need some time to care for yourself. Make it a habit to indulge in activities that feel good several times a week if you can.

·   Learn to Be Okay with Uncertainty - There are times when the unplanned moments in life turn out to be the best thing that ever happened to you. Maybe you didn't plan to go out to the bar that night, but if your friend didn't drag you to it against your will, you might never have met your future partner. Maybe you worried about the change in management at your workplace, but several weeks later you realize how refreshing the new ideas introduced by the management could be. Uncertainty is always going to be part of what makes life go up and down, whether you like it or not. Since we can't change this fact, do the next best thing and learn to accept that uncertainty is part of yours (and everyone's) life. Accept that you don't know what the future holds, because no one does. The only difference between you and them is that they're not worrying about it. Uncertainty does not always equal the worst-case scenario outcome. Acceptance doesn't mean your worries are going to go away. It means you're choosing not to let it stop you from living your life.

·   You Don't Need to Be Afraid of Risks - Sometimes you need to take risks to see change. You need to be willing to make big moves that others are not. You need to take a leap of faith if you want to make a considerable difference. That's what everyone else is doing, and if they can do it, you can too. They do have their worries and concerns, but they manage it by doing their due diligence and arming themselves with information. Knowledge is going to be your best defense against your unruly imagination. When you've got facts to fall back on, it's easier to challenge your mind when it tries to convince you otherwise.

· 	You Can Handle Discomfort - It's time to remind yourself of that fact. You're bound to have handled several moments in life when you were pushed beyond your comfort zone. You survived then, and you will keep on surviving because that's what we do as people. We adapt, we survive, we overcome discomfort and we thrive. Discomfort means you don't like what you have to do, but it does not mean you can't do it. You probably can. You would prefer not to, but you can.

· 	Stopping the Clock - A lot of worries are fueled by a sense of urgency. They believe they need to do something fast and they need to do it now. Feeling like you always have to race against the clock is the surest way to spike your stress levels. Beat the urge to race against the clock by focusing on one task at the time. Always think in moves that put you one step ahead and closer to solving the problem. Remember that you can't do anything when you're in a panicked or stressed out state. Remember that the terrible outcome you're thinking about probably won't happen. You can handle anything if you set your mind to it. There's no need to put a timer on everything, pace yourself and take it one step at a time.

·   It's Okay to Cry About It - Cry when your emotions feel like they're too much to handle. Crying is not a sign of weakness, it's a way of releasing your emotions. Let it all out, don't suppress. Cry about it for a few minutes of you feel emotional. As long as you feel much better afterward, that's all that matters.

Chapter 2 Looking At Things From A New Angle

Whether it is conflict or decision-making, understanding how things appear at a different angle is beneficial. It helps to be interactive and inclusive. Differences may exist between people and partners in a social, family, or working relationship. When this occurs, it is necessary to do less political strategizing and more thinking of different angles for solutions. Being able to look at things from a new angle requires three skills: perspective-taking, perspective-seeking, and perspective-coordinating.

1) Perspective-taking

Perspective-taking is a critical component of communication. Depending on where we stand, the way we perceive facts and their meaning can be very different. The perspective we adopt influences what we consider obvious or obscure, central or peripheral, and present or absent. Just like the way we perceive the physical world, perspective influences the human experience in the social world. If we can see things in a different angle, from the perspective of another person, we can have responses that are more constructive rather than several strong disagreements. At the least, we can be careful in what we do or say in challenging times to avoid escalating negative outcomes.

Mistaking perspective-taking

When we are trying to look at things from a different angle, we should avoid two pitfalls: overconfidence and uncritically considering another person's view as valid. More often, we get overconfident that we are succeeding in viewing things from a different perspective. Remember a time your friend was displeased with the birthday gift you bought her or doubly upset for not understanding her troubles. The fact is that you may have tried to take their perspective but ended up with a mistaken one.

Studies have revealed that people are often inaccurate when they infer the thoughts and feelings of another person by observing the behaviors and facial expressions of that person. More important, people become overconfident that they finally managed to get a different perspective right.

Another common pitfall is the idea that most people treat another person's perspective as valid, thereby using it to solve a problem. When our perspectives are based on wrong assumptions, the effect is missing the real issues or misleading conclusion. An example is a leader making judgments on an incident with the assumption that he/she had access to the critical information for decision-making. However, if the assumption is wrong and not questioned, then the judgment could end up solving an integrity issue when the real one could be information quality.

2) Perspective-seeking

To successfully view things from a new angle, you also need to have the skill of perspective-seeking. Once one is able to listen to other people's perspective, they should be able to judge whether it is right or wrong. This skill involves understanding another person's point of view on a particular point or circumstance. It is about being curious to hear and learn more about other perspectives.

The greatest trap on this skill is reaching out to people with a similar point of view that you have in order to validate a hard decision you plan to make. It is important to listen to people who may have a different opinion from yours and discover new things as well as potential blind spots.

3) Perspective-coordinating

Once you can take different perspectives and seek them out, you need the perspective-coordinating skill in order to utilize the information you received. Perspective-coordinating entails observing what lessons are available from the other perspectives. This skill helps us to understand other people we speak to and the impact of our final decisions on them. Also, perspective-coordinating enables one to understand the contributions of different viewpoints in every situation and how they help in decision-making.

How to Radically Look at Things From a New Angle

Perspective-taking not only brings empathy in our social relationships, but it also brings in compassion and mindfulness of the people we connect with. Below are the ways through which you can successfully view things in a new angle by considering other people's views.

Think of others

When we are in the presence of other people, we naturally begin to think about what they are thinking. We observe their behaviors, such as where they are looking, what they are doing, and their body language. This observation helps us to determine whether we can be comfortable around them or have further association with them. If you think about other people and feel comfortable around them, we begin to think of how to connect with them. The information you get by observing others will prompt you to speak up in a conversation and get to learn their perspective.

Regulate your emotions and empathy

Taking perspective depends on our ability to share emotions as well as the capacity to regulate our emotions. In order to be effective with other people, we must understand the things that trigger us so that we can refocus ourselves in time on what is happening to others. In regard to empathy, we should try to understand what other people would do in a particular situation rather than what we would do.

With stronger empathic accuracy and emotional regulation skills, you can be successful in considering different perspectives. The skills can help you to predict expectations, intentions, and attitudes of others, which may be different from your own.

Reading others correctly

Our perspective-taking guides are the emotions, which help us to read and learn people. Our eye and brains help us to track the behaviors of others and determine what they are feeling or thinking, then determining their intentions and motives. By being sensitive to other people, you will be able to sense their possible emotional changes, which can help in gauging how to successfully show up in the interaction.

4. Interpret words

Most people do not speak directly, which often requires that we infer the mean of what they are trying to say. However, this always creates a lot of room for misinterpreting the message, particularly those sent via email or text. By accurately interpreting what the other person is saying, you will be able to make the right decision on what to say and avoid conflict.

5. Respect the existing differences

To take the perspectives of other people, we need to have the maturity to respect the personal beliefs of others and respect their knowledge. If we disrespect others, they will separate themselves from us and avoid sharing their constructive ideas with us. It is important to be highly attuned that people hold different beliefs and world views, and as such, remain open-minded and respectful as we interact with them.

6. Be interactive

We must interact with people in order to develop empathy and learn from their ideas. Interactions are made possible by asking questions and listening to find out the concerns and experiences of other people. When individuals engage in naturalistic connections, they can tell each other what they truly think rather than what the other person wants to hear. As a result, this opens up doors to learning new perspectives.

Quality interactions build social cohesion, promote mutual trust, and reciprocity norms. Over time, these traits motivate people to see things from others' perspectives, promote collaboration, and facilitate conflict resolution.

7. Strike a balance between subjectivity and objectivity

To empathize with the perspective of another person, you need to actively adopt that perspective with subjectivity and emotions. But note that empathy should be accompanied by certain level of detachment to maintain objectivity for effect perspective evaluation. Detachment refers to the ability of an individual to step back from an idea in order to see the bigger picture. This way, we can learn other people's perspective and apply them adequately.

Chapter 3 Negativity As A Cause For Anxiety

Anxiety and panic attacks are all products of ingrown negativity. When you allow negativity to take full control of your life, it is impossible to keep a sober mind.

What is Negativity

Negativity is a constant expression of pessimism or criticism. The expression of pessimism only shows the thinking process of a person. When a person is negative, he/she places limitations on every aspect of life. They allow their minds only to see the negative aspects of life. Although life has some negatives, life also has plenty of positives. Unfortunately, the human mind tends to lean towards the negatives most of the time. If you wish to live a happy life, overcome anxiety, and attain success in life, you must live a positive life. Negativity will only worsen your fears and worries. If you become pessimistic about issues, you may never see the beauty of the world. You will constantly worry about what is about to happen and pay attention to negative occurrences in life. It is important for you to train your mind and change the perspective of life.

In the human mind, there are three factors that will determine whether you are a positive person or a negative one. What you do, how you react and how you respond to issues determines whether you are negative or positive. First, you should be able to tell whether you are negative or positive. Knowing where you stand as an individual will help you start monitoring your actions and reactions.

A classic example of negativity is the proverbial say of a glass with water at the halfway mark. One person will say that the glass is half full while another will say that it is half empty. One person is so much concerned with the emptiness of the glass to such an extent that he/she cannot see the fullness. If you have a negative mind, you do not see the positives in any matter. As a result, your actions and reactions to circumstances show negativity.

Negativity can be summed up by the acronym AIR.

A- Action

I- Inaction

R- Reaction

These three words define a negative person to the detail. When it comes to action a negative person is always reluctant to take action. Most negative individuals pay too much attention to the risk than to the gains. This then leads to taking negative actions most of the time. They will take longer to take any action but when they eventually take that action is to the negative side.

Inaction means that the negativity causes a person to stand on the fence. When important actions have to be made, a person who is negative may stay away and refuse to be involved in any way possible. This lack of action often leads to the matter escalation from bad to worse. We have mentioned above that if you worry so much, you do not solve anything. The best way out is to take action and wait for the result. Due to negative thinking, most people have missed important life opportunities. For instance, if you happen to like a certain girl so much, but you keep on fearing to approach her, she will eventually be taken by another person. By approaching the girl you like, you unravel the Pandora's Box. There are only two answers to expect. Before you ask her out, there are 50/50 chances that she will say yes. But if you do not ask her out the only answer you can get is a no. Being pessimistic or negative only blocks your life from achieving many things. You close your gates to success and block away people who wish to get into your life.

The reaction aspect of your life also determines whether you are negative or positive. If you are a positive person, you will react positively to circumstances. A person who is positive does not have a lot of problems when dealing with negative emotions. Even if you are told something negative, you try to find out the positives out of the situation.

For us to live a happy life there is a need to adopt a positive life. You need to stop thinking in a negative manner and start focusing on the positive aspects of life.

What Causes Negativity

When you were a young kid, you probably had big dreams and visions. When you ask grade one kid what they want to achieve in life, you will be amazed at the limitless targets they have set in life. However, as people advance in life, they start reducing such expectations. This helps us understand that the limits we have in life are caused by life experiences. Since a child has fewer experiences, he/she expects that everything will turn out okay in life. However, as we go through life and experience realities, we start setting limits to whatever we can achieve. We start setting limits on our potential and eventually, most people lose hope and result to living life as it comes each day.

If you want to see success in your life, you must learn to maintain your limitless mentality. In this , we will be looking at some of the ways we can reset your mind back to the limitless state. The mind of a human being is designed to crave success. Every person should desire to touch the skies and achieve the best in life. You should not let life experiences breed negativity in your life. Some of the life experiences that lead to negativity include.

Failure: The biggest cause of negativity in life is failure. As mentioned, a child has so many dreams and ambitions. However, as people grow up, their dreams and ambitions start fading away. One of the major causes of dreams fading away is failure. You start realizing that although you wish to be a doctor, your failure in exams may not allow you to be a doctor. This leads you to block away the possibility of being a doctor. If failure prevails for a long time, a person will eventually stop trusting their ability to achieve anything. Consecutive failures may kill your self-esteem and make you feel as if you are not worthy of anything in life.

However, those who make it in life are individuals who have a resilient spirit. If you give up on your dreams because of failure, you may never see happiness. First, you need to deal with every situation that tries to cultivate negativity. Do not allow negative thoughts and emotions to occupy your mind. When you fail at something you may feel worthless or stupid. Do not allow such thoughts to occupy your mind. You must constantly remind yourself that even if you go through failure, it is only a matter of time before you succeed.

"Only those who dare to fail greatly can ever achieve greatly." - Robert F. Kennedy

It is the individuals who know the value of failure who keep on trying and trying. Some of the luxuries we enjoy today might not be in place if those who came ahead of us would have given into failure. The Airplane took so many trials and errors before it was finally designed. The same case applies to electric bulbs and other scientific innovations. This shows that if you wish to succeed in life, you must prevent failure from creating negativity in your life. If you fail at doing something, start over again. One failure experience gives you sufficient knowledge and changes your perspective.

Betrayal: The other cause for negativity is betrayal. Betrayal is a situation where a person you trust goes behind your back and does something harmful. Betrayal can cause devastating emotional pain. The pain associated with betrayal must be dealt with immediately to avoid the case of negativity. If you do not let go of the pain caused by betrayal, you may harbor bitterness in your heart and develop negativity.

The negativity associated with betrayal leads to someone never trusting others. If you choose to focus on the betrayal for long, your mind is made to believe that all people are dangerous. You start looking at all your friends and family members with a negative perspective. If the issue grows deep in your mind, you eventually consider every person in your life an enemy. Lack of trust with colleagues and family members is negativity. These negative thoughts block your path to success. You cannot succeed or be happy if you live around people you do not trust. If you keep on thinking about the harm they can do to you or your family, you may develop fear and start experiencing anxiety and panic attacks. Anxiety starts from such a simple point. Only one person betraying your trust may lead to trust issues and a lot of emotional pain.

Rejection: Rejection is another emotional situation that can lead to pain and bitterness, which may eventually develop to negativity. Those who develop pain and bitterness from rejection leading to negativity do not understand the value of their worth. It is common for a person to be rejected. Although we all crave to be loved and needed, it is normal for a person to look at you and think that you are not worth. One important factor you must understand is that you do not need the approval of people to be yourself. You do not need to be complimented to be beautiful. You are awesome and amazing in your own way. You are authentic and no one else can be like yourself. Therefore, be ready to accept those who accept you in your natural beauty. At the same time, do not pay too much attention to a person who has rejected you. Why do you waste your energy trying to fit into the life of a person who thinks you are worthless? The best way to deal with such a person is to work hard and show them that you are better than they think.

Unfortunately, individuals who are not strong enough mentally and emotionally allow the words of people to breed negativity. If someone rejects you and you start feeling worthless, useless and valueless, you allow that person to win. You should not give anyone too much power over your life. Accepting that you are valueless only makes the person who rejected you right. The truth is that you are amazing in your own ways. In your natural state, you are still attractive to many others. Choose to focus on those who appreciate who you are and what you want.

Loss: People who suffer from negativity always think that any investment they make will end up in a loss. This is mainly because they have suffered losses in life. Profit and loss are a normal part of life. You cannot expect to make gains without ever making losses. In any business, profit and loss are part of the vocabulary. Even the most established firms in the world have to suffer losses from time to time. Understanding that loss is an integral part of life will help you to get rid of any negative thoughts. When you experience loss, you must learn to tell yourself that "next time I will succeed". If you experience loss, get afraid and run away from the business, you may never succeed in life. Learn to look at your loses in a positive way.

Losses that lead to negativity include loss of money, business, friends, and loved ones. If you lose someone too close to you, your entire life may seem meaningless. If you find yourself in a position where you do not see the value of life due to loss, you must encourage yourself and stand up again. Do not allow the one-loss you have experienced in life lead to multiple losses.

Abuse: The other reason why people develop negativity in life is abuse. People go through different types of abuse from childhood. It is important that you get rid of any pain of abuse; both physical and emotional. Emotional abuse wounds stay with a person or a very long time. If you wish to live a happy life, without fear, worry and panic attacks, you must get rid of any painful abuse memories. One of the best ways to release such pain is by talking about it. If you have suffered pain when growing up and you find it difficult to trust or to love, you can deal with the pain by talking about it. You can talk to your spouse, friends or close family member. This way, you open your mind and your heart about the issue and release the pain.

Both physical and emotional abuse can lead to pain which eventually grows into negativity. For instance, if a girl was raped by a close family member, it becomes difficult or such a child to trust anyone in life. You may grow up fearing everyone around you. If you have been through an abusive case, you may find yourself looking at people with questionable eyes. The intentions of every person in your life become suspicious. It is your duty to ensure that you get rid of any negativity from your mind and you choose to focus on positivity at all times.

Chapter 4 Defining Co-dependency in Relationships

What is Co-dependency?

Co-dependency can be defined as an abnormally excessive psychological or emotional attachment to a partner (in any relationship), usually one with an addiction or disability; be it emotional, mental or physical. Co-dependency often appears to be a highly traditional relationship standard, one of caring for your partner and putting their needs before your own. Many co-dependents exude the virtues of nursing, support, love and affection and maintain these traits to be the very reasons to remain with an addict and as such continue to nurse their addictions in an effort to find that thing that makes them feel complete.

One note that should be made now; is to understand where co-dependency traits originate. Most frequently these traits are learned due to a long history of addiction, poor self-image, abuse and the lack of emotional fulfillment in one's formative years.

Some Characteristics and Examples of Co-dependency

Firstly, co-dependency consists of numerous traits, attitudes and behavioral characteristics which make it easy to identify in relation to other relationships. Co-dependency often starts out in a relationship when one partner develops and addiction to the traits of their partner, be it their partners own addiction or abusive behaviors and traits. When this happens, one partner becomes the enabler of the other, usually this happens gradually. In some relationships the addicted party finds their way gradually into recovery while the enabler is left to cope with the emotional and mental scars, patterns, and discontent or resentment of their relationship. Some of the most distinct examples of co-dependency are when one person is abnormally addicted to the negative behaviors or addictions of their partner to:

1) Alcohol:

Living with an Alcoholic:

Sarah* is 25, she is successfully employed as the managing editor of a large magazine revolving around the entertainment industry, and in her off time she picks up work as a freelance writer for other industry publications. Her romantic life is deeply founded in her belief that even when in a relationship women should always remain independent. Sarah spent many years working with a therapist before making these decisions in regards to how she wanted her life and relationships to work. While Sarah would appear to be a success story, this is only because of her past and her ability to overcome co-dependency.

Just two short years ago Sarah was an intern working at a highly regarded local weekly paper. She was on the road to success; this publication had a reputation for only employing the most talented young journalists from all parts of the country. It was an honor for Sarah to get this position, and it was the first step in her dream to escape the small down monotony that she had known all her life. She had high aspirations for herself and saw herself as the shining star of journalism that every famous publication wished to hire. Shortly after starting her internship, she met Alex. He was older, more mature than the boys she had wasted her time dating, charming, and attractive. Sarah was smitten. Of course so was every other young female working in the office, drawn to his wit and wisdom no one seemed to notice the slight hint of whiskey on his breath. It was destined that Sarah would start dating Alex after they spent time working closely on a new formatting project and no one was surprised when they moved into his apartment a few weeks later, many of the old foundation staff had seen this happen before. Sarah was head over heals in love with Alex, spending all of her time taking care of him, showering with love and catering to his every whim. She made sure that he had all the luxuries he was used, and was determined to ensure that she was always there for him when he needed her. It didn't take long before his addiction crept out and took over their relationship, it was a rocky road and Sarah was far from prepared for the wild ride she was about to embark upon. Sarah was positive that if she provided him with regular company he would chose her over his love of whiskey. Slowly she became drawn to the care he needed when he was drinking, she liked the dizzy speed of life when they were out on the town. It all seemed manageable at first.

Then, one day, after returning home from the office, Sarah came home to find the house unlocked and Alex was no where to be found. It was in this moment that things suddenly became very real and inescapable. Alex's drinking had nearly turned deadly, the diagnosis was grim and Alex was faced with the decision to stop drinking altogether or he would surely die. It was a medical nightmare, for three months Alex found himself fighting his inner demons while in treatment. Sarah spent her days trying to hide her own drinking and her nights pacing the floor alone with her own liquid demon feeling lost and empty without Alex there to keep her spirits up soon she was drinking more than she ever had when Alex was home! In time Alex home, he has a new lease on life, and was ready to take on the world while Sarah was now trapped in the grasp of the buzz she had come to be so familiar with since he moved in with Alex. Reality was Alex had successfully stopped his relationship with alcohol...Sarah did not. After several weeks of pleading with Sarah to get the help that she needed and being told to mind his own business Alex broke things off and asked Sarah to move out. Sarah felt as if she had lost everything, her best friend, the man she loved, her home, and the very world itself. So, she drank until her own health seemed to be at risk. Eventually, someone cared enough for Sarah to insist that she get the help she needed to enter rehab herself and to remove her addictions from her life. It was a hard road but in the end, Sarah was free!

Alcohol addiction in co-dependency is cited as one of the most prevalent cause and effect indicators of problems in one's relationship. Statistics show that the wives of alcoholic men account for the highest percentage of co-dependent individuals in society. Why? At its core a co-dependent relationship is defined by one partner being addicted to the negative behavior of another to the detriment of the entire relationship.

We all have the right to live our lives as we wish, partaking in the things that makes us happy or feel good, but we must always keep in mind that there is always a cost involved for the abuse/overuse of anything. The reality of this cost is often forgotten by the co-dependents as they grow in their addition to excess as well as to the need to be with one another for fear they would not survive alone!

2) Drugs:

Living with a chemically addicted partner

She was seventeen, and the memories that were soon to be made in college looked as if they would be the best moments of Elianna's* life. She had always dreamed of finding her college sweetheart and being swept up in the social scene of a big University. Life was not going to let her down, and once they met love was quick and overwhelming for Elianna and her crush Victor. They met during the second week of school at a fraternity party, in no time at all they were engaged and living together soon after. But there was a dark side to college life and in no time Elianna found herself struggling to keep her head above water, it was at this point in Elainna's life that she was introduce to the boost you could get from taking ADD meds when you didn't have the affliction. By the end of her freshman year she knew all the tricks to buy these prescription pills from other students. Everyone seemed to be doing it, friends and strangers got high all hours of the hours of the day. During her second year Elainna found the high she could get from pot and ecstasy were more than she could get from prescription meds. Life was constantly getting harder to cope with everyday. As with any other addiction the use of a stimulant drug to cope will soon not only impact your own life, but the lives of those around you.

This impact would soon find its way into Elianna's life and that of her friends and family. College didn't get any easier with the help of even the strongest of drugs and Elianna was forced to leave college her grades had slipped and she no longer had the money to pay for her classes without the assistance of student loans that required good grades. Shortly after this Victor left her. She attempted to get a job and support herself, but her continued addiction led her to spend more than she earned each week. She knew that the drugs she was ingesting were harmful, but she didn't care, they were her escape from the painful reality of her life. No matter how momentary the escape was. When things started to look the grimmest and the high was no longer enough to hide the darkness around her Elianna sought to end it all with a needle in her arm. Elianna thankfully did not die, thanks to her best friend whom she had decided to call and say bye. Because of this friend Elianna found her way into rehab where she stayed for two years. Elianna has found the calm that she needed to escape from all the hardships of her past. She owns her own home, and has found the strength to start her own business raising organic crops from her small farm. Rehab, opened her eyes to many things. She knows that as always she has the right to decide what she will do with the moments of her life.

3) Sex:

Living with a Sex Addict

Alaine and Dan had dated for four years, it was the longest relationship she has ever had, and when he broke up with her she was devastated. She had never imagined that life would be anything but the perfect picture she had painted for herself. Growing old with Dan was all she hoped for. When he was gone Alaine found she missed the emotional and physical bonds that they had once with Dan. She envied her friends carefree dating life, spending time with men she had just met. Some she would see again, but most were merely one night stands. They often talked about the topic of dating and how sex was not necessarily something to be denied simply because you had not met your soulmate. Then one night at a party, she decided it was time to throw caution to the wind and she hooked up for the night with a cute guy she'd never seen before. They found themselves at a sleazy hotel where they spent hours having the best sex that Aliane had ever had. The thrill had hit its mark.

Aliane was overjoyed, she couldn't thank her friend enough for her words of encouragement and shared every aspect of the wild trip she had started upon.

A month went past and another, then one day Alaine woke up body aching feeling used and not having recalled having been with a man in a room that she didn't recognize. Many men had found their way into their bed, and many had tried to have a relationship with Alaine. Each one was met with the same response…"It's been fun, but it's just not going to work. I have needs that you just can't fulfill"

Aliane was caught up in the thrill; it didn't matter where she got it man or woman. Sometimes multiple partners in one night were still not enough to fill her needs. No more was it just the thrill of the sex, it was the thrill of getting caught, or the carefree thrill of having unprotected sex because it felt better for her and her partner. She threw caution to the wind and refused to use contraceptives of any kind. It was no longer a rush to have sex with as many people as possible it was a physical need that must be met. Until the day she woke up exhausted, unable to move, coughing racked her body and blood ran from her nose. It took all she had just to crawl to the phone and call an ambulance. The paramedics found her passed out on the floor. After three days in ICU the diagnosis was grim, Aliane had contracted AIDS and was now suffering from pneumonia. Forced into a life of celibacy depression soon took over her life and she was faced with months of therapy to feel whole again.

This is not to say that sex is bad, it is far from it. The mutual enjoyment that comes from intercourse is one that should be shared with someone you love. A healthy sexual appetite in a relationship is a good thing, it is an emotional bond unlike any other, but being smart and practicing safe sexual practices should always be a priority. For your own mental health, never be a slave to your physical desires!

4) Parent-Child relationships:

Co-dependency in Children

One of the most natural and potentially most harmful of co-dependencies exists in the relationship between a parent and child or child and a sibling. The addiction in this case does not owe itself to a substance, but instead to a sense of security of one's family. Dependency of a child upon a parent for the fulfillment of emotional stability during our youth may seem to be sweet or endearing to a parent. However, in the view of a child, this is a fear that arises from the worry of being abandoned by their parent or being unable to satisfy the dreams the parent has for them. This can lead to issues of homesickness, panic-attacks and depression for a child causing him to fear they may be alone forever. The child may find that they are incapable of making their own decisions regarding the simplest of things, or frozen with fear when out of the parent's presence during their formative years.

Co-dependency in Parents:

Another form of co-dependency in the Parent-child relationship is one in which the parent forms a dependency upon their child, and the child the enabler. In case of many parents, the mistakes lie in acts of over-protectiveness. This is not to say that a parent should not be protective over their children. However when afraid to permit their child to take an escorted flight to visit their grandparents in a distant city because of the chance that the flight may crash this is a sign that the parent may be exhibiting overprotective tendencies as they are overly concerned over something that is in all probability unlikely to occur. This behavior and anxiety should be with counseling and therapeutic care. Sometimes parents stress too much over their children's career plans as a resultant idea of their own life experiences, hence, the child loses his own identity in their desire to please their parent. Many a times, parents are the ones who neglect a kid's innate desire to choose a career out of his own interest, which leaves the child filled with resentment and the urge to rebel against the career in which they find themselves.

Children do not come with handbooks, and parents are not given users manuals to aid them in the proper care and raising of a child. If you become a parent remember that your child is a separate entity from yourself and should be allowed to grow as a unique individual separate from you. Teach them to live their lives not yours, and show them the tools they will need to be successful in life.

5) Mental or Physical Disabilities:

Mental Disabilities:

Living with an OCD-Person

Dave had just taken a position in a new office when he happened to meet the girl of his dreams, Elissa. Dave and Elissa met and found they shared a crazy view of life at an office Annual Party. Dave had recently suffered a break up and was in a rush to begin dating once, and Elissa happened to be just the spark that drew him in. Elissa moved in with Dave little by little and at every step of the way, Elissa showed signs of discomfort until Dave allowed her to rearrange the apartment to her standards. Within a few short weeks, Dave's apartment had a new order to it. "A place for everything, and everything in its place." Dave learned the things that triggered Elissa's anxiety and he himself began to become overly critical regarding cleaning the already pristine floors, straightening the wrinkles on the bed and organizing the freezer just so. Elissa and Dave had a huge fight and she moved out. There were no attempts at reconciliation, however, Dave was convinced if he was able to achieve the results she desired she would come back on her own accord. The biggest change in Dave came when he became so brutally obsessed with cleaning and organizing the apartment that is consumed his entire life even keeping him from going to work. His obsession became so intense that getting Elissa back was his only thought…but that speck of dust in the air kept him from her.

His colleagues visited him and talked to Dave, he promised them he would come to work, but nothing of the sort happened. Dave continued to find a sense of calm only when he was able to clean. One day, his friend Maria visited him and managed to drag him to a psychiatrist. The doctor was confident that in time they could work out a plan to resolve Dave's disorder. The therapy worked and Dave showed a significant change in the span of less than a month.

OCD in regards to cleanliness is one of the many virtues that make a person become alert or enlightened about the order, hygiene and healthy aspects of things, irrespective of their size. The obsession can be about anything and co-dependency clearly states that obsession because of anything on an abnormal basis leads to a bad behavior of craving or needing that affects mentally.

Living with a Schizophrenic

Another potential trait of a person in co-dependent relationships is the aspect of feeling that they are the sole support of the disabled. One in which the responsibilities of caring for a partner is what drives the other partner to excessively provide for the needs of the other. The feeling is more than love as it is started mainly based on a sympathetic bond. The enabler provides compassion and love in unbiased proportions so much so that the survival of both becomes impossible without the other. Love is merely a façade in this case.

Schizophrenia for example should be treated as quickly as it is discovered. A schizophrenic needs professional help not just heavy dosages of compassion and coddling. As time goes on and the disorder is not treated the enabler finds themselves to be resentful of the dependent in their life and depression is sure to seep into their life. Eventually, there comes a point when the schizophrenic seeks out medical help. The enabler however, does not. This is a very dangerous position to be in.

Living with a Bipolar or Suicidal Partner

Perhaps one of the hardest aspects of any relationship to over come is when one partner is overcome by such a strong mental or emotional state that they are unable to explain or even comprehend what it is that is going on in their own life. In the case of a Bipolar or Suicidal partner the emotional state of the partner is unpredictable and when left untreated...deadly. This forces the enabler to become an interpreter for their partner. Trying to understand their partner's needs and emotions while also maintaining a sense of sanity for them both is debilitating.

In case of Physical Disabilities:

Living with the paralyzed victim of an accident is one of the many situations that is most often portrayed in films and televisions. Impairment during an accident renders the partner to instantly take on the role of enabler mode. It is a fine line between healthy and co-dependency. The physicality of the events is usually genuine from both sides. However, the trauma can induce certain behavioral changes in the victim as well as the partner. Certain outbursts of anger, verbal or physical abuse, withdrawal and isolation all occur and create distress in even the strongest relationship. .

There are many examples of how an enabler's life can be stressed even long after the dependent is out of the picture. The focus of their lives while on some level is natural and ordinary other aspects are the result of past relations in which they participated in co-dependent behaviors rather than those of genuine love. Some of the practical examples of co-dependency can be seen in human characteristics such as seeking behavior, looking for love, friendship, companionship, the desire to care for someone in need, drowning their emotions in food, and eventually humility. In addition, a co-dependent chooses to vent out this specific frustration and undue pressure using many other ways. Some of them can be heavy, but everything can be managed if help is sought sooner.

Chapter 5 Common Problems Related to Procrastination

By now we are completely aware of procrastination. None can say that they don't know procrastination because they do and they would have experienced it at some point. Some people tend to identify the problem of procrastination, and they eventually treat it. But some others don't! They need support and ideas to overcome procrastination, and it is not something to be ashamed of. It is okay to ask for help and guidance. But the ones who get delayed to identify procrastination face a lot of problems because of procrastination. If you feel like you are procrastinating, make sure to take the necessary steps to overcome the problem. Don't wait until the last minute to treat it because it is dangerous. However, let us discuss some of the major problems related to procrastination. Here we go:

Losing precious time

If you have heard motivational videos done by Jay Shetty, you'll know how important time is! We waste time as if it doesn't have value, but it is the most valuable thing in the world. If you think about the time you wasted, you will not feel good about yourself. The worst part is when you realize that you've grown up so much, yet you have not changed a bit or even improved at all. You are still in the same place where you were. When this hits you hard, you will not be able to move, and you'll be frozen in the spot wherever you are! I understand it can be one of the terrible feelings. You might regret, but you can't take back the time that you spent.

But it is okay, and it is never too late. You can start now. You can change it now! Think about the changes that you must incorporate and keep following them!

Avoiding opportunities

You might have gotten many opportunities, yet you put off them for tomorrow. The most common word among procrastinators is tomorrow. But little do they know that it is causing so many destructions. When you realize that you have missed so many great opportunities, you might want to slap yourself as hard as you can. But what's the point?

Remember, you are still getting opportunities. Yes, you have got the opportunity to change, so make use of it!

Not meeting goals

This is going to thump you, imagine for how long you have been missing your goals. You might have had a strong need to achieve the goals, but then, procrastination happened. When you think about it now, you might feel the deep-cut pain in your chest. But you can still achieve your goals. You just have to uncover the reasons for procrastination and then, get rid of them.

Missing the ONLY job

You may not have missed out on your job, but some people have missed their job because of procrastination. Perhaps procrastination is not a trait that employers want to see in employees because it will be a threat to the company's performance. Missing deadlines often and not attending meetings are not great things! You shouldn't procrastinate, it doesn't matter whether it is work or home.

Lowering self-esteem

Low self-esteem can be one of the reasons why people procrastinate. But the sad part is that your self-esteem goes down even more, when you put off work. You start questioning your capabilities. Moreover, you will lose confidence in yourself and become vulnerable. Low self-esteem is a significant threat to your life, so find solutions to overcome this problem.

Poor decision-making

When you become a pro at procrastination, you become a novice at decision making. When you procrastinate, your decisions will be based on the things that you believe right. Your emotions will take a toll on you at this point. Eventually, poor decision making will make your life miserable.

Damaged reputation

If you don't do something that you haven't promised, it is okay. But when you say something that you will never do, it is going to be dangerous. For example, you keep missing the deadlines and give great excuses, so how far can you take this lie? Do you think you will still have the job after missing too many deadlines? I don't think so. The client may have a bad impression on your reputation. Thus, through procrastination, you are damaging your reputation as well. You will witness that people stop sending you tasks or people stop contacting you for important work because they know you are not the right person. You will always be considered as someone who'll not be able to complete a task in a given time. You don't think that a damaged reputation is easy to handle.

Risking your health

Another common problem associated with procrastination is that of stress, fear, anxiety, and many other health issues. If you think health issues related to procrastination ONLY concerns your mental health, well, I'm sorry to say that there's more to it. Even though mental health issues are also severe, you will end up hurting your overall body by procrastinating. Like we earlier, there are chances for you to get different types of diseases if you don't work accordingly. Basically, due to procrastination, you tend to work day and night without actually giving enough importance to your body. Do you really know how vulnerable your body is? Do you know how carefully you should handle your body? If you know all these, you wouldn't even think of procrastination. Typically, procrastinators don't spend much time in analyzing these things. Instead, they do their job –wasting time!

Sacrificing your happiness

You will not understand the factor of sacrificing happiness until reality hits you hard. You might often be procrastinating, but you get the work done in the minute, and that makes you think that you can are capable of doing something when you want to do it. There is a clear cut difference between determination and procrastination. Determination is when you don't delay the work for the second time. Basically, by completing the work at the last moment, you are losing a lot of things. For example, if there is a family event planned, you will not be able to attend it because you are too busy working. Likewise, you might sacrifice your happiness whenever you procrastinate. Procrastination is not only unhealthy but also makes you unhappy!

These are just some of the common problems related to procrastination, but there are many other severe problems. You are lucky, you have decided to change, and that's why you have reached the last page of this book. I hope you change for the better and have a productive life!

Chapter 6 Accept Yourself

One major reason why women overthink is because they have been taught that it is not okay to accept themselves and love themselves as they are, largely based on the fact that they have been taught by society and the media that nothing they do is appropriate. As a result, women begin to feel as though they cannot accept themselves as they are because, if they do, they might begin to engage in behaviors that could possibly result in them not being liked or accepted by those around them. This type of fear-based belief system can lead to women feeling as though they have to criticize everything about themselves in an effort to continually stay focused on the steps that they need to take in order to fit in and stay accepted by their peers. Of course, the truth is that there is no reason why anyone cannot be their true self, as there will always be people who like us and people who do not like us and it has nothing to do with our ability to meet society or the media's standards on how women are meant to fit in.

This particular strategy is excellent for any woman who is overthinking for any reason, although it will be particularly more powerful for women who find themselves consistently overthinking as a result of fear or shame. If you find that you are someone who regularly overthinks as a way to process your worry about whether or not you will be good enough, worthy enough, or valuable enough for the people around you, this strategy is an excellent way to stop that behavior in its tracks. When you learn to accept yourself, you stop worrying about whether or not other people accept you because you feel self-validated and self-confident, which ultimately ends up putting you in more positive situations where overthinking and worry are not necessary.

When you learn to accept yourself, overthinking can be overcome because you no longer feel as though you have to attempt to work so hard to remember everything that you need to do in order to fit in or be accepted by those around you. When you accept yourself, you do not need to be accepted by everyone else because you can trust that everyone will either accept you and like you as you are, or they will not accept you and thus they will not be an important part of your life. This type of adjusted belief system empowers you to feel safe in being who you truly are which, unlike attempting to fit into society, is extremely easy to remember because you just have to be.

Accepting yourself is typically not something that can be done immediately, as truly and completely accepting yourself will take continuous practice and a great deal of healing efforts being exerted toward the topic itself. However, you can begin to accept yourself immediately in each moment as you discover that you are overthinking about things by simply adopting the affirmation "I accept myself" and then following through on it by choosing to accept yourself in that moment. For example, say that you are stressing out over going to a meeting because you are afraid that the person will not like you for some reason. Instead of overthinking every little detail and attempting to fit yourself into the confines of what that person says you need to be or do, you need to choose to accept yourself as you are. This way, if the person does not like you for any reason it does not matter because you accept yourself enough to trust that if this meeting does not work out you will come across something better and more reasonably suited to who you are in the future. Then, when you begin to experiencing overthinking thoughts that run along the lines of "will they like me?" you can simply say "I accept myself" to combat those thoughts.

The more you choose to accept yourself, the less you care about how other people see you because you already accept yourself as you are. If you go on a date and someone does not like your hair, or your sense of humor, or your interests, for example, you will feel confident that they are simply not the right person for you. Rather than attempting to mold yourself to fit into the image of who they want you to be, which is typically what overthinking attempts to achieve, you can simply accept yourself and trust that those around you will accept you to. The ones that do not accept you do not need to be around you any longer, it is as simple as that.

Find Reasons to Be Grateful

Overthinking as a result of fear can lead to individuals forgetting about the good things that they have in their lives, which can lead to greater feelings of worry and fear, which then leads to more reasons to overthink. If you find that you are regularly finding yourself trapped in overthinking spirals that stem from feeling afraid or not being able to see what good things you have in your life, using gratitude as a strategy to put an end to your overthinking behaviors is a powerful strategy. Gratitude has the capacity to shift our focus and leave us feeling more empowered and at peace with our lives, which can enable us to then have the energy and motivation required to accomplish anything that we desire to accomplish in our lives.

The easiest way to use gratitude as a strategy to overcome overthinking is to begin thinking about all of the things that you are grateful for anytime you find yourself overthinking and feeling trapped in thoughts that reflect why you are not worthy, lucky, or deserving of a better experience. You can use gratitude in any way that you want, although there are two ways that allow for gratitude to easily be incorporated into any experience that you may be having in your life, and any timeframe that you have to contribute to overcoming your overthinking pattern in the moment. If you have a shorter amount of time, using a shorter strategy with clear outlines is a great way to begin infusing your mind with more gratitude and reminding you what you have to look forward to and what you have to offer the world around you. If you have more time, using gratitude in a freehand way to support you in remembering every single thing that you have to be grateful for until you are feeling better is an excellent opportunity to overcome your overthinking behaviors.

If you need to use a shorter and more structured gratitude practice in your day, choosing to affirm five things that you are grateful for to yourself anytime you begin to feel fear or unworthiness arise in yourself is powerful. When you recall these five things that you are grateful for, make sure that you not only slow down to remember what they are but that you also actually express and allow yourself to feel a moment of gratitude for each one. For example, if you are grateful for a moment that you shared with your Grandma before you flew back home, taking a moment to affirm that memory, recall that memory, and genuinely feel into the gratitude that you now experience is important. By completely anchoring in those feelings of positivity and gratitude, you allow yourself to shift your mood which, then, shifts your thoughts. This works by not only distracting you but also by reverse engineering your behaviors by using your emotions to adjust your thoughts, rather than allowing your presently unproductive thoughts adjust your emotions.

If you have more time, or if you want to incorporate gratitude into your daily strategy for overcoming overthinking behaviors, giving yourself the opportunity to actually write down everything that you are grateful for can be powerful. Much like a brain dump where you write down everything that you are overthinking about, you can use this time to write down everything that you are grateful for. Because you are turning your thoughts toward something positive with this experience, you do not necessarily need to set a timer to stop yourself after a certain period of time, although you can if you feel that you need to or want to. However, simply writing down every single reason why you are grateful until you feel that you have expressed gratitude for everything that you are grateful for can be extremely powerful. This allows you to align with feelings of gratitude, positivity, hope, optimism, and other symptoms of gratitude so that you can begin feeling more at ease with yourself and your thoughts. Then, anytime you find yourself overthinking during the day, simply recall something from your gratitude list and spend some time leaning into those thoughts so that you can feel more at peace with yourself.

Chapter 7 Principal Frequently Worries

If you have ever been diagnosed with any anxiety disorder, there are chances that you know what it's like to live with constant worries. It is worth noting that feeling of being unease and being focused on your current difficulties in life as well as potential problems may cause issues that affect an individual`s life. In other words, the feeling may range from the fear of upcoming events such as weddings to the safety of a family that might be far from one`s sight. It is also important to note that people who struggle with anxiety-related conditions are negatively affected by their worrisome thoughts. Many worrying conditions can be exhausting and might increase when stroked with more anxiety and fear about the future. The art if worrying is dangerous in the sense that it makes one worried about their safety, and one might have difficulties to unwind or even relax. Also, the art may contribute to sleep disturbances as well as extreme conditions of insomnia.

It is worth noting that worry has a direct link with anxiety. In other words, people who are associated with this condition have been in one way or another been diagnosed with panic disorder. Individuals who have a panic disorder frequently experience some worries. For instance, one might be worried about losing a friend and end up in the chaos in the later future.

If you keep worrying from time to time, you need to prepare for future events in advance and avoid any confusion that might set in. For instance, you might have to exercise or engage in physical activities that will help you release the tension you have over the upcoming events. You need to organize your home as well as the office and watch a funny movie that will help you recover from the feeling of being unease. You may also engage in an activity such as drawing or writing and try to get support from your colleagues. For instance, you may need to hear a perspective of another person that might help you change your minds.

The other aspect that is worth doing is sharing. For instance, you may spend some time sharing your worries with someone. A good friend will help you overcome the situation and help you mind off the concerns that might be affecting you. Also, you might have to network with other individuals who will help you take some time and relate with others. In other words, the art of sharing becomes more effective and efficient when shared between individuals why have ever had such experiences.

Practice Relaxation and Self-care Techniques

It is worth noting that most of these signs of worry are linked to one`s mindset. Thus, if you need to release the worrying tension that you might be having effectively, you may need to practice some of the effective relaxation techniques. For instance, relaxation techniques tend to serve the purpose of improving one`s art of thinking, and it helps lower the tension that one might be having. Some of the relaxation techniques that have proved to be effective include yoga, meditation, as well as progressive muscle relaxation. Some of these techniques don't require a company or rather, a lot of individuals for them to be effective. Some like Yoga can be practiced at the comfort of your living room and achieve excellent results. However, it is good to determine some of the activities you need to do in life. The aspect is essential in the sense that it allows one to for the future and be effective in attending all the events without any tension.

Panic Attack

Scholars, as well as a psychiatrist, have identified that many people have developed one or two panic attacks in their entire lifetime. It is worth noting the problems go away when the stressful situation or the cause of the distress disappears. However, if an unexpected panic attack faces one, the problem seems to persist and might stay for long before one resumes to their normal state. Although the condition isn't life-threatening, there are cases where frightening tend to affect the quality of life significantly. In such a situation, treatment tends to be effective.

Some of the worst situations about this panic attack are that there is intense fear that tends to develop and affect the way a person lives. There are cases where people fear developing some of these attacks and end up improving the symptoms of the condition. One of the alarming signs that are common in such situations includes dizziness, extreme headaches as well as the feeling of unreality or somewhat detached from the rest of the society.

Causes

There are no known causes of a panic attack. However, there are a few factors that are associated with this condition. Such factors include genetics, significant stress, a temperament that is more sensitive to pressure or somewhat prone to some of the negative emotions that one may develop. It is worth noting that the condition may develop suddenly without any warnings at first. However, most of these sighs are triggered by a particular situation.

In most cases, when the situation fast attacks one, the rate of breathing rises sweet, and the heartbeat rate also increases. However, some risk factors may expose one to frequent panic attacks. Such factors include family history, significant life stress, a traumatic event such as a sexual assault as well as substantial changes in one's life, such as divorce or an addition baby in life. Smoking, as well as excessive caffeine intake, might be a significant cause of this condition.

Chapter 8 Principal Panic attack Disorder

A panic attack might involve sudden or terrifying feelings that strike without warning. It is worth noting that theses strikes can be profound and may occur at any time. One of the most frightening situations about this condition is that one may have a notion that they have a heart attack. Some victims feel dizzy or as if they are going crazy.

In most cases, the terror and the fear that a person experiences during a panic attack might be proportional to the situation they are experiencing. The anxiety of developing a heart attack or a panic attack among such individuals worsens the situation. A lot of people with panic attack experiences the significant symptoms of a racing heart.

It is worth noting that most panic attacks are brief and lasts for about ten minutes. However, the condition may worsen and persist longer, depending on the striking cause. Researchers have identified that people who have developed the state once in their life-time have higher chances of developing the disease in their future. A person is said to have developed a panic disorder when one experiences repeated episodes of a panic attack. In most cases, the fear of developing the condition worsens the situations as one end up developing a heart attack, which can be life-threatening.

One of the significant conditions of this disorder is extreme fear and anxiety that is unpredictable at times. The panic attack is relatively common, and it is affecting more than 6 million adults in the world today. It is worth noting that women are concerned with a more significant percentage than men does. The aspect is linked to the fact that women are more fearful than men.

Researchers haven't identified the primary cause of this disorder. However, some people have developed the biological vulnerability of being attacked by this condition. Most of these victims are associated with significant life changes such as getting married or having a child when least expected. Also, the art of starting a new job as well as living in a new place might be a significant cause of developing the condition. It is worth noting that people who have developed this condition are most associated with other conditions such as stress. If the situation isn't arrested in the light moment, one may suffer from depression and several attempts of committing suicide due to fear. Other victims who are found of alcohol turn out to be addicts.

It is fortunate to note that a panic attack is a treatable condition. Psychotherapists have been using medications, either singly or in combination with multiple counseling sessions that have been offering a successful means of curbing the disease. If necessary, some doctors prescribe anti-anxiety medications as well as anti-depressants or anticonvulsants drugs that tend to have some anti-anxiety properties. The art of treatment is essential in the sense that it allows one to protect from developing heart condition as well as other associated conditions such as depression. Thus, if you have been experiencing episodes of a panic attack, make a point of seeing a doctor and prevent the disease from worsening.

Chapter 9 Mind Decluttering and Emotions

When there's clutter around, it can be a little distracting. Even though you might not consciously be thinking about it, your eyes still see it, and on the smallest level, that is still taking up some brain power as you have to ensure that you are processing everything you see in front of you.

If you have stacks of magazines, a guitar you never play, and other unfinished projects lying around, it is going to make it more challenging to focus. You will still think, somewhere, even if it is in the darkest depths of the back of your mind, that you should be giving attention to this project. Even though you might not actively think, "I really need to start retaking my guitar lessons," your brain still thinks about that guitar, which could trigger other subconscious thoughts.

When you are not actively clearing your mind, it can be a lot harder to learn new things or pay attention to what you should be focusing on in front of you. Just as a cluttered home can keep you distracted, so can a mind that isn't correctly processing thoughts. Sometimes, we might obsess over an idea and let that become our main thinking point throughout the day. However, we all have to take a moment and make sure we hit the "reset" button every once in a while to give ourselves a clear-thinking pallet.

Think of your mind like a chalkboard. You write one thing down, maybe a quote. Next up, you have to write a formula, so you do so in the blank space underneath. You continue to add things but never erase anything. Eventually, you are not going to have any room to write anything else. If you don't properly work through what was already there on the board and clean it off, it will still show through the next thing you might write down. You want to ensure that you are giving your brain a chance to become completely clear. Wipe it clean like you would the chalkboard to make sure that you are not letting yourself become too distracted.

The benefits of decluttering your mind are clear. You will be able to see things in a new light. You can start to have a better sense of the things that are most important in your life. You will no longer have to worry about the small stressors that might have been distracting you before.

When your mind is filled with stressful thoughts, it only makes it easier to think of more stressful things. You can start on a pattern of stress that is seemingly endless. You will think of one stressful thought, and then remember all the other pressing issues that you have to attend to all because you have started down the road of stress. Before getting into what mental clutter looks like and how to overcome it, identify your clutter so you can have a sense of the things that you need to free your mind.

Signs of Mental Clutter

Mental clutter is sometimes common to see, but when that's all we know, it is hard to realize just how cloudy our brains can be. When you are in the middle of your mental mess, it is going to be a lot harder to pull yourself from this! Clutter can be like quicksand, whether it is physical or not. The more that you have surrounding you, the easier it is to sink deeper and deeper into it.

When you hold onto specific thinking patterns, then it can be harder to create a newer headspace. If you want to free yourself from chronic stress, it is time to pay attention to the thought processes that are keeping you stuck in the past. Overcoming stress and managing it in a healthy way will involve starting a new in your life.

You won't be able to think the same way that you do now if you want to move onto a more stress-free life. You have to create a new headspace, and that will start with cleaning out what is there already.

When you always feel sad and isolated, it might be a sign that you are letting other thoughts beyond reality dominate your thinking patterns. It is easy to feel lonely even when we are in a crowded room, but you have to remind yourself that you are not alone. We all have own mental anguish that we hide from others, so just because someone isn't expressing their pain in the same way that you are, this doesn't mean that they can't relate to the emotions that you might be feeling.

If you feel as though you might be struggling beyond the anguish anyone else feels, then you might be throwing yourself what some refer to as "pity parties." When we start to convince ourselves that "no one understands me," or that others aren't able to feel pain as deeply as you do, then you are the one that is isolating yourself. We all feel pain differently, but everyone has their problems, struggles, and agony. If you are poor and see someone wealthy thinking they have it all, then even this is a misguided way of thinking. Just because someone is wealthy doesn't mean they are free from pain, just as someone poor doesn't necessarily have to be depressed. Money certainly makes life more comfortable, but as you can see, it is the perspective that matters the most.

When you struggle to make a decision, even something as simple as what to eat for dinner, you might be having an issue with mental clutter. The smallest tasks can be rather challenging to overcome when you are mentally cluttered. Work stress can make it hard to decide what to cook for dinner, and before you know it, you are arguing with your partner in the frozen at the grocery store because you can't decide between two different types of pizza. The issue here isn't the pizza. It's the unmanaged stress that has carried over – the mental clutter.

Uncertainty and having no faith in the decisions we might want to make can present their challenges for us (Morin, 2018). We all second-guess ourselves and reflecting on our choices can be important in helping us prevent ourselves from making mistakes in the future. However, it can get to a point where we have zero faith in ourselves and can't make a decision just because we're so insecure about picking the right answer!

If you keep up with consistent fantasies well beyond your present reality, then you might need to do some mind-cleaning. It's easy to daydream while waiting in line at the DMV or at a party you were forced to go to in the first place. Long thought out fantasies and frequent episodes of escaping to a different world in your mind is a hint that you might have some mental clutter that needs to be let go.

These are some other cognitive disorders that can present challenging thinking patterns. When you become aware that these are negative or unhealthy thinking patterns, it will be easier to recognize them and work through them.

Cognitive Distortions

A cognitive distortion is a pattern of thinking in which reality is twisted to suit a perspective that you might already have. When you are stressed, it can be easy to see the world through the eyes of someone experiencing multiple stressors. You will imagine only negativity as opposed to being able to think about the positive aspects of your life. Our minds are focused on reinforcing thoughts that are a bit negative.

Why we think in way is up to the individual. Not everyone experiences these cognitive disorders, but once you do, it can be easier to start to create a web of negative thinking. Rather than seeing the positive reality of some situations, you might start to pick out only the bad things that happened to validate these perspectives.

Our brains are self-preserving, so it can sometimes be natural to try and reinforce some of the things that we believe to be true. Your brain wants to protect itself at the end of the day. This is why we work, so we can eat, provide shelter, and do other things necessary for our health. It's why we love, so we can feel better, and get the support needed while making an emotional connection with others. Your brain wants to make sure that you are taken care of and that you are protected in all aspects. We do still think of others, but a lot of the patterns of thought we have come from a place of maintaining our perspective.

When you have a negative perspective, your brain is then going to be more likely to validate that rather than challenge that. Think about a friend who comes to you discussing issues with a relationship. The first thing you would probably do is support them, tell them that they're right about their feelings and things like that. You might challenge them, later on, to see things from the other person's side, but it is natural first to find ways to validate these thoughts. Your brain will then do that. So, if you come home from work and think, "I hate my life, today was terrible," then you will think this the rest of the night. You will see a sink full of dishes and an empty fridge and get discouraged. You'll look for something to watch and think to yourself how there is never anything good on TV. You'll keep validating the idea that today was terrible rather than looking for ways to think about how today was great.

These things – the sink full of dishes, an empty fridge, and a lack of something to watch – these can all be bad things. They can also be good! A sink full of dishes means that you enjoyed the food in the past and had a plate to put it on. An empty fridge means that you can store food when you want. A TV means that we can watch amazing shows with nearly unlimited resources for finding new things to watch. The reality of the situation exists, and you can decide to either see the positive or the negative perspective.

"All or nothing" kind of mentalities can cause mental confusion. As humans, we often label things because this is easier for us to understand. You can label things as either black or white, big or small, plentiful or scarce, feminine or masculine, good or bad. However, if we only allow ourselves to see the world in two ways like this, it gives us an "all or nothing" mentality. If you are late to work once, you might label yourself as a bad worker or someone irresponsible. If someone is rude to you once, you might label them as a bad person. If you watched one episode of a new TV show and didn't like it, then that means the entire show is bad. This mentality limits us and rather than helping us to understand something, this extreme labeling keeps us from having intellectual discussions. To combat this thought process, notice when you are labeling something. Have you given it a fair chance? Could it be something in the middle?

When we make assumptions and overgeneralize an entire situation, this can keep us thinking negatively. Assumptions are another way that we might try to take a mental shortcut to understand something better, but again, all that happens is we end up limiting our intellectual capabilities. Your assumptions might often be right, but don't feel the need to make them all the time. This can lead to a stressful life if unmanaged.

It's always good to be prepared, but sometimes, our brains get good at picturing the worst possible thing that could happen. Try instead to imagine the best case. Then, the truth will likely be somewhere in the middle. Sometimes we think so negatively because it is a way to prepare ourselves. Rather than being disappointed that things didn't turn out in our favor, it is easier to never get your hopes up in the first place. The issue here isn't the perspective, it's the situation that determines your emotion.

Let's take the example of inviting a particular friend to your birthday party. Maybe that friend flakes frequently and you can't trust they're coming just because they say they are. You could choose to be optimistic and hope they come. You could be pessimistic and assume that they aren't coming because of their past. Or you can deal with reality as it comes, and accept that if they don't come, you'll be fine, but if they do, you'll be even better. Being either angry or hopeful are strong emotions, and you are not wrong for having them. However, you might fall into a pattern of always being angry that could damage you in the long run.

Giving control to anyone but ourselves over our actions and decisions can be a cognitive distortion. Another person might do something harmful or damaging to you, but this doesn't mean that they control your emotions. You might think, "They made me feel mad," but they didn't make you punch a hole in the wall. Separate the emotion from the action, and you will start to see reality more frequently and easier.

A weighted mind, believing that something is fair or owed to you, can be a challenging way of thinking. We are owed our fundamental human rights from other people, but the idea that we aren't living justly can damage our perspective. Fairness is measured in a complex way. Just because someone has something you don't doesn't mean that things aren't fair. You might have something else that they don't have. Don't measure fairness as a black and white 50/50 scenario. It is much more complicated than that.

Placing blame on others is a sign that you might be thinking with cognitive distortions. It might be someone else's fault for an accident that occurred, but they can't be blamed for everything that happened after that. You could do this if you wanted, but in reality, it is only going to hold you back. You are giving power to them rather than taking it for yourself, and if you do this too often, you will end up feeling helpless.

Once you become aware of these distortions, it starts to get a lot easier to overcome them. You won't be able to switch the way that you think overnight. The first step is recognition, and from there, you can work to think a little clearer and brighter every day. Here are a few more methods of clearing your mind that will help you to de-clutter.

Ways to Clear Your Mind

This is a good place where becoming aware of your thought patterns through the use of a journal. You should start to keep track of all the cognitive distortions that you had. What thinking pattern did you notice, and how are you able to turn it around?

Remember always to question reality. How would someone else see this situation in the same way? How might you be able to describe this pattern to someone else? Challenge your thoughts and gain a sense of what is happening rather than basing everything off your perspective.

Let go of old thoughts. This doesn't mean that you have to forget everything that ever comes into your mind. You should merely be emphasizing working past those emotions and creating new feelings within yourself to heal and overcome.

Forgive people. You have an unlimited amount of storage for your memory, so you won't need to worry about running out of space to remember. However, if you don't forgive, that means you think about what happened consistently. Forgiving doesn't mean pretending it didn't happen. It means that you are letting go of the hurt that you felt at the time so that you can move on. It means finding a new emotional balance in which you can grow and heal rather than festering in what happened.

Remember to focus on small goals right now. You might have a million ideas in your head for things that you want to do, but you should focus on one thing at a time. It will be easier in the long run to focus on the most important tasks and completing them before moving on rather than doing it all at the same time. This can cause mental clutter and confusion that can make it more challenging to move on.

Remember that your situations that you experience now, no matter how bad, will play into building the person that you will become. Even the most hurt that you have ever felt in your life still taught you something. The most significant pain you've ever experienced managed to give you clarity in some way. It won't always be easy to see, especially right after the pain is experienced, but all that you live through is important in creating the person that you are right now.

Ask yourself what this mental clutter has ever done for you? How has being distracted and caught up on other thoughts kept you from becoming the person that you want to be? What things might you have been able to do in your life if you would have been able to think freely and clearly?

Take time to do mindless activities, such as playing a game, watching a bad movie, or just zoning out and listening to music. Not every second of your day needs to be packed with stimulating content. Give your mind a break and a chance to reset, and you will find that it becomes easier to manage stress as you do so.

Chapter 10 Avoid Distractions

Are you easily distracted? Are you consumed by your thoughts and worries to the extent that you cannot concentrate? If the answer to the question is, 'YES', then it is time for you to learn to be in complete control of your actions, thoughts, and emotions in order to stay focused.

Importance of Having Focus

The focus is the gateway to all types of thinking. Your perceptions, reasoning, learning, memory, decision making and problem-solving all rely on your ability to focus. If your worry and anxiety are hampering your ability to function, then something really needs to be done. Especially if you are expected to work at a certain optimum level, you should not allow distractions to impede your personal and professional growth.

If you are making worry a recurring feature in your life, then you are setting up yourself to fail. It is imperative to avoid distractions, because:

Distractions disrupt your thinking. Lack of focus due to distractions affects your efficiency. Your mind is constantly bombarded with worry and anxiety, so you have the tendency to procrastinate your own work. When your mind is wandering, you end up wasting time and your productivity suffers. This compromises your overall output.

Distractions compromise the quality of your work. If you're used to performing at a certain level, your performance and productivity will be adversely affected if you allow distractions to disrupt the process. A certain level of commitment is required to accomplish the desired quality and quantity of output. In order to achieve it, you need to overcome and avoid distractions.

How to Be More Focused

Gaining control over your distractions is important. You are not being asked to forget all your worries or ignore them. What you are being advised, is how to be strong enough to function despite the problems in your life? Everyone has to deal with their own share of worries; what matters is how disciplined you are, to be able to work around them.

The following are some winning strategies against distractions:

De-clutter your mind. When your mind is cluttered, it is preoccupied with all kinds of garbage. So many things are going through your mind that you cannot focus on the task at hand. Prioritizing usually works because it allows you to dedicate a special time to a given task and temporarily pushes aside other things.

Learn to disconnect. Your head is spinning with thoughts and if that's not enough, your surroundings are abuzz with all kinds of other technological distractions that signify the incoming of an email, text message, call or social media notifications. While it is important that you stay connected, do not be afraid to disconnect, even for a while. You will be more productive when you keep yourself away from technology - especially if the messages only press harder on you.

Clean your work area. Your area of work is supposed to be free from any clutter. Look at your desk. Are you feeling cramped up in your area because of too much litter on your table? Physical clutter is just as disruptive as mental clutter, in terms of productivity. If you want to lessen your anxiety, evaluate your workspace and rid yourself of all the junk that holds no importance to your current task. If it is not going to improve your efficiency, it should not be on your table.

Create a plan. If you have the tendency to drift away from your goal, you will need a plan to get back on track.

A plan is a detailed process that you need to follow. If you drift off course, you can refer to your plan and get back on track.

Stop over-thinking. People have the tendency to be obsessed with their worries, expecting that thinking might lessen the intensity of their worries. But worries do not thin out, however hard you think about them. In fact, worries affect you more if you allow them to creep into your system. You cannot 'think' your worries and anxieties away, so you just have to stop. You have to let them go in order to carry on with the things that you have to do.

Distractions come in all forms. People have their own types of distractions and they will attack in varying intensities. You have to be strong enough to push all your distractions aside, no matter how pressing they may seem.

The 4 Ps of Productivity and Efficiency

No matter how big the conundrum you are going through; no matter how problematic your life seems to be, but you must go on, you cannot let these things consume you. In terms of work and productivity, your most significant weapons are the 4Ps:

Performance – Always focus on what needs to be done. You have to understand what is being required from you so that you can give it your best. This means that you have to focus on what needs to be done to dismiss the distractions that linger in your mind.

Process – Every function to be done correctly follows a specific process. It is a step-by-step procedure that needs to be undertaken and you have to focus on this process to ensure that you produce good results. Paying attention to every detail in your work takes your mind off all the clutter and helps you to focus and prioritize.

Present – Sure you have troubles and worries threatening your life right now. Unfortunately, you also have a task to perform so you should refuse to be distracted by all these things. You have to focus on what needs to be done now, so you have to push away everything that hampers your functioning and productivity. Later on, when you have time, you can devote it to your worries. But right now, you have to perform and you have to stick to the process.

Productivity – You have goals, deadlines and demands that you need to meet. A responsible individual will not be satisfied with half-hearted work. A conscientious person values productivity above everything else, so he will block all unnecessary thoughts that will not contribute to the fulfillment of his project.

Are you always overcome by the clutter in your life? You have to realize that everyone has to deal with distractions and they come in various forms. Your worries and anxieties do not have to creep into your life to destroy your functioning. Remember the 4Ps— performance, process, present and productivity. Regardless of how important your worries seem, you have to focus.

Chapter 11 Stop Trying to Please Everybody

"No one can make you feel inferior without your consent"

Eleanor Roosevelt

Insecurity can eat up anyone. Sometimes, even the most stable person can be overcome by what others have to say, whether it is about their performance, physical appearance, attitude and so forth. The truth is that people always have something to say about others, and if you consistently find yourself in such a situation, it can be really demoralizing resulting in worry and anxiety. Trying to please everybody is a difficult task. If you don't realize how much you're harming yourself by trying to please others, you will end up exhausted.

Are You Worrying Too Much About What Other People Think?

Are you always trying to please other people? Feedback is good. It is good because it highlights your strengths and weaknesses according to how other people see you. It is good because it gives you room for improvement and development. Unfortunately, when one is unable to process negative feedback, it starts eating them and leads to low self-confidence and low esteem.

Do you worry too much about what other people think?

Do you end up doing things because that is what other people expect you to do? It's not wrong to take advice from others. A lot of important decisions in your life could've come from someone else—but it doesn't mean that you have to always do what other people expect you to do. When you worry too much about what other people want you to do, you end up living up to their expectations to the extent of sacrificing your own happiness. This causes you to resent your own choices and eventually cause worry and anxiety.

Are you afraid to speak up your mind? Are you worried about going against others? Why are you so worried about what other people will say? You should always stand up for what you believe is right and should not be afraid of what others will say. Everyone is entitled to their opinion, but you should not let their opinion affect you. You should not let other people's opinion worry you. As a matter of fact, you should learn to stand up for what you believe is right.

Are you struggling to make decisions? When you worry too much of what people are going to say or think, it is difficult for you to make decisions because you're considering too many things. Instead of thinking of what's best for you under the circumstances, you are also worried about what others will think about the decisions you make. Of course, your decisions will affect others too, and it is good to consider these external factors; but you should not compromise yourself just to please others. You should never put yourself in a bad situation, just to appear in the good books of other people.

Do you have the tendency to avoid people? In an attempt to elude people's opinions and reactions, you may just choose to hide. It's easier this way because it saves you time and effort, but this doesn't really deal with the problem. The truth is that you cannot hide forever. You will encounter these people and no matter how hard you try to avoid them, these things will catch up with you.

Do you refuse help? Are you afraid of asking for help from others because it shows your vulnerability and weakness? When people have so much to prove to others, they always want to "win". They refuse to accept assistance from anyone even if they are in need because it admits defeat. Everyone needs help from time-to-time. You should be strong enough to accept your weakness without feeling defeated or inferior. Also, why are you killing yourself trying to achieve perfection? Nobody is perfect. The person you are trying to impress is not perfect, either, so relax and do not be too harsh on yourself.

It's never easy to impress people. It is always difficult to find something positive in the negative that people say about you. Criticism and negative feedback are always going to stab you no matter how prepared you think you are. So if you think you can avoid these things, you need to ponder over again.

Therefore, instead of hiding from it, you have to learn to face it head-on. If other people's opinion brings you too much worry and anxiety, something needs to be done about it right away.

Stop Worrying About What Others Say

You are human, therefore you are concerned. You are human, therefore you feel pain. Other people's opinions bring you much worry and anxiety because you are human and you care. It's not really a bad thing, but the resentment you feel towards others is not healthy. As a matter of fact, it can destroy relationships.

The key is to create a new mindset. You cannot control what people will say and how they will react to the things you say or do, but you can control how you react to them. Have you ever wondered why people's opinions bother you so much? Is there really something wrong about what people say or are you just being too hostile about it? Do you think you are being too sensitive or too critical about yourself? Are you sure you are being attacked or is there something wrong about how you perceive things?

If you want to stop worrying about what people think about you, change your mindset. Introspect and question your own thoughts, because maybe you are looking at things the wrong way. Moreover, endeavor to be more self-aware, so that you can be confident of the kind of person you are without needing validation from someone else.

Someone's opinion about you does not depict the sum-total of your persona, so stop trying to please everybody. You are only bringing yourself unnecessary anxiety.

Chapter 12 Mindfulness

As we approach the end of this journey, I hope that by now you have learned a great deal about yourself, your emotions, and your personal way of thinking on a daily basis. Hopefully, you have become intimately familiar with the areas and experiences in your life which trigger overthinking. The interruption technique we went over earlier is an invaluable tool for breaking the cycle of overthinking, and cultivating new, healthy habits on a daily basis is a great way to replace those old useless habits.

There is a lot to gain from taking a breath of fresh air outside in a park or reading a book rather than inundating your mind with pointless and depressing social media and news feeds. You've addressed the negative influences in your life, from magazines to friends, and you're starting to feel like a new person ready to realize your dreams. I also hope you've learned something about your chosen occupation or career path and, though this is probably the hardest area to make changes, I hope that you've either reaffirmed your joy and satisfaction with your current job situation or have taken steps towards finding a new path that is specific to your skills and what makes you happy.

The final skill I'd like to introduce in this is all about mindfulness. There are three forms of mindfulness I would like to discuss, though they are all closely related and are a part of each other. Mostly, I want to mention all three because they are often interchangeable, and if you do not recognize one, I'm sure you will have heard of another. They are mindfulness, meditation, and positive thinking.

Now, it's true that you may think positive thinking is not the same as mindfulness and meditation, but in a lot of ways, I do consider positive thinking to be a form of meditation and I will explain in a bit. First, let's define mindfulness a little more clearly.

Mindfulness

When I say the word "mindfulness," many people often think automatically of the phrase "paying attention." If this is what you thought of, you're not wrong! Paying attention to what you're doing, your environment, and how you're feeling is an important part of practicing mindfulness. But it does go deeper than just paying attention, and for most, it is more difficult than it sounds.

Mindfulness is a practice of being present, not just for a minute or two, but throughout the day, every day, over the course of your life. The goal is to maintain mindfulness all the time, though we all accept that we are not computers or robots and there will be times when we lose focus or our minds fill up with other emotions and feelings that take us away in reaction to life events. A parallel can be drawn with a religious mindset. In the Christian mindset, followers accept that they are human and will make mistakes, while at the same time doing their best each day to maintain a sinless, righteous, and faithful existence. Just because we know we will make mistakes; doesn't mean we don't try. And this is why the long-term effects emotionally, spiritually, physically, and emotionally are well worth our efforts. So, let's look at what mindfulness has to offer us and then we'll learn how you can integrate the practice into your own life.

Think about how you feel after you successfully banish a needless or hurtful thought and replace it with a new, positive one. It makes you feel good, right? And it also gives you a sense of clarity, like a big mess has just been cleaned up from the floor of your mind. The same thing happens when we learn to practice mindfulness. Only with mindfulness, there is a bonus.

Practicing mindfulness consistently leads to a feeling of potential, of hope, and of looking forward with a fresh pair of eyes. You are moving forward with a clear mind and you are taking stock of each second that passes you by. So, when I talk about a feeling of potential and looking forward, I'm not talking about looking forward to the next day or weekend or month. I'm talking about moving forward, step by step, minute by minute, feeling and seeing everything around you and feeling each moment as it passes. There is a feeling of happiness and satisfaction that follows because you are getting rid of the thoughts that have no use for you in this moment. And your mind is thanking you.

Your heart and soul are thanking you. There is so much to sense and be grateful for here and now. Mindfulness is all about bringing in your perspective to these close quarters, small-scale way of thinking, and in the process, the whole world opens up to you.

So, how do you start practicing mindfulness? Well, the biggest task here is going to be honing the skill of focus. But there's good news. If you've been able to practice the interruption technique and replace your negative thoughts and emotions with positive ones, then you've already done a lot to cultivate this skill. Focus comes from the mental effort of sharpening your thinking and scaling it down to a single task without letting your mind wander all over the place to things that are not helping you perform that task. As I've before, you don't want to fall into the trap of trying so hard that this exercise becomes a chore and a source of worry for you. Everyone who is new and first being introduced to mindfulness is going to move forward and improve at a different pace because we are unique human beings. And that's perfectly ok. As with everything else in this book, the key is to take small steps at a time.

A good exercise in practicing mindfulness is simply to go outside and experience nature. Go to an area of a park that is generally quiet and take a seat at a bench or a picnic table. Take a few deep breaths and quiet your mind. Give yourself a minute or two to accomplish this. While you begin focusing your mind, listen to the sounds going on around you, the dogs barking, or the wind blowing through the trees. Feel the breeze on your face or the heat from the sun beating down on you. Feel your body in space. Make sure you are sitting in a comfortable position. Close your eyes as you begin. Then, as you start to appreciate and focus only on what's around you, slowly open your eyes. Look around and take in what you see without forming thoughts around them. Again, this may not come naturally, but gradually with practice. Appreciate the beauty around you, whatever it is you see. If you don't have a nice park to go to, you can do the same exercise in your own backyard or neighborhood. Listen to the birds or the kids playing down the street. Try to focus only on sensations without forming thoughts about them or letting your mind wander. As you make time to practice mindfulness just for a few minutes each day, you will start to notice that it is getting easier the more you practice.

Meditation

A discussion on mindfulness follows naturally into a discussion of meditation because they are closely related. To me, they are part of each other while indicating different practices.

Meditation, for many people, translates to practicing mindfulness throughout each and every day. To others, meditation means a dedicated space of time each day or week that is used for formal meditation practice from a specific school of thought or philosophy. For example, Zen Buddhism. I will mention a few different styles of meditation but will be discussing Zen in particular because it is the form with which I am most familiar.

The same exercises you've practiced in nature can be applied to a practice of meditation. Since most people associate meditation with the image of sitting in a quiet room with your eyes closed, let's look at how you can start practicing meditation in your own home by following a few simple steps.

Depending on your physical ability, find a comfortable position where you can sit with your back relatively straight. Your arms should be relaxed at your sides, and your neck should not be strained. A simple Google search will go through the more formal sitting structure if you are interested in this, but for right now, we will take a casual approach to the physical technique and focus more on what's going on inside your mind.

When we mindfulness, we talked about sensing the world around you and concentrating only on what is happening to you in the moment. Meditation is similar, except that, in the discipline of Zen meditation, the goal is not to restrict one's thoughts, but instead to resist sticking to individual thoughts as they enter and exit your mind. The core emphasis is still to focus on the present, but the philosophy of Zen is to not restrict the mind but to instead free the mind and let it remain fluid while returning consistently to the present experience.

To illustrate this, have you ever caught yourself or a friend has caught you zoning out, staring blankly in front of you, while your mind drifts and starts to have a dialogue with itself regarding something you said yesterday or something embarrassing you might have done years ago? The thought process has taken you completely out of the present, and now you are lost in a replay of moments that have already happened, things that cannot be changed. But still, you dwell on those moments as mistakes and worry about what people think about you, while in reality, they probably don't even remember those insignificant events. Sound familiar? We all do it. The ultimate goal in meditation is to avoid those sticky thoughts that try their best to take us out of the present and into the past or the future—spaces that either cannot be changed or that we cannot predict. The brain likes to know things and form patterns in an effort to predict and make sense of our lives. But we can get wrapped up in this to the point that we miss life as it is happening in the present.

Zen is all about acknowledging the wandering nature of the mind but also accepting the core principle of impermanence—everything changes, even the thoughts in your mind. Dwelling on a single thought or feeling or emotion is useless and irrelevant in an impermanent world and will only hold you at a standstill.

This may not make perfect sense yet, and if you need to start with the absolute basics, go back to that phrase we brought up in the beginning of this —

Just "pay attention." Look around, feel yourself in space, listen, appreciate. That's really all you need to focus on to get started. As with all of these positive habits, you will soon form a new addiction to the positivity that mindfulness offers. After this point, meditation will follow naturally.

As I mentioned, meditation can take many forms and you should not feel like there is one right way to meditate. Many practice mindfulness and meditation through movement to music called dance meditation. Other people, including Zen Buddhist monks, practice "walking meditation." Movement often helps regulate and soothe the mind as we introduce patterns of movement that flow just like the free-flowing of our thoughts. Whatever your style and preference, just remember why you're practicing in the first place, and there is no "doing it wrong."

Positive Thinking

Positive thinking links right in with the thought technique where we were interrupting negative thoughts and introducing positive ones. But with positive thinking, the idea is to cultivate the positive thoughts first, instead of waiting and using them as a reaction to negative thoughts. This is another practice that will look different from person to person. It also should not be an overwhelming concept that discourages you from trying it.

Simply put, positive thinking means you practice waking up and thinking about each day as a fresh, new, unpredictable day rather than dreading what you think you know is already going to happen. Nobody knows the future, and even if your routine seems pretty set in stone, when you form the habit of dreading something each day in connection to work (which is something I hope you've already addressed!), then you close yourself off to experiencing surprising things or things that would give you joy. You may recognize what I'm talking about with an example. Think of Mr. Scrooge from the classic Christmas tale, "A Christmas Carol." It's Christmas eve and there are children laughing and playing in the snow, people shopping and sharing Christmas cards and talking joyfully with strangers. But then there is Mr. Scrooge trudging through the snow toward his office, already determining that Christmas is a terrible time and there is no happiness to be found in it—only loss of money. Because he's already determined that he will not be enjoying Christmas, he is unable to open his heart to the joy going on all around him.

Similarly, when we wake up and dread what is going to happen that day, we become blind to the events that would offer joy and surprise and happiness. Did you know that people receive subtle signals not to engage or talk to you when you are upset or unhappy? Think of all the fun spontaneous conversations you've had at work when you arrive in a good mood, positive, and open to whatever the day will throw at you. Let this thought be a motivation for you to try cultivating positive thinking every day, at the beginning of the day.

Cultural Backing for the Effects of Positive Thinking

You may or may not remember the phenomenon of the "law of attraction" as it was popularized through releases like The Secret. Many believe that positive thinking actually works to attract positive events and effects in your life when you practice consistently. You've probably heard the saying, "if you put your mind to it, you can accomplish anything." This is what positive thinking and the law of attraction is all about.

It may help to journal about your experience as you practice this skill. Think of a goal for your life. Maybe it's a goal you've had for years and years, or maybe it's something you just thought about today. Write down your goal in your journal and write a little bit about what accomplishing that goal might look like for you. Perhaps you see yourself with a family and friends at a big party as you celebrate a promotion, or you've set aside time for a family vacation to the Bahamas. Maybe you're visualizing yourself having lost 30 pounds in that new bathing suit you've had your eye on for a long time. Whatever your goal, the idea here is to write out the experience with as much detail as you can imagine. Really make it real in your mind, then write down what you see.

Next, you'll want to write down the steps on the pathway toward your goal. Positive thinking is a powerful tool, but to make your goal a reality, you're also going to need to put in the work. What do you need to do between now and next year that will help you reach your promotion? What plan do you have in place to follow in order to lose weight safely and in a way that you can sustain?

If you watch movie awards shows, you may be familiar with the speech many of the winners give in which they attest to visualizing and thinking about their dreams for years before they actually achieved what they wanted to achieve.

If you let yourself get depressed and convince yourself you can never accomplish something, then you definitely will not accomplish it. Practicing positive thinking will naturally carry you closer and closer to your goals, because you are motivating yourself, consciously and subconsciously, to be ready for those opportunities that you would probably miss with a negative mindset. Just like Scrooge and his blindness to joy, it is possible to wrap yourself so tightly in negativity that you don't see an opportunity right in front of you.

Practice positive thinking and mindfulness in small steps each and every day, and soon it will become easy and natural to continue. The joy and freedom that comes with practice like this is something your mind and body and spirit will begin to crave. Just like when you exercise and your body thanks you with all those positive feelings from endorphins and a sense of accomplishment, your mind and body will thank you with positive feelings for the future and it will become hard to resist the pull of positivity.

Don't take my word for it. If you work hard to cultivate and maintain these positive changes in your life, I'm positive you'll hear about it from those closest to you as they witness the changes happening. It may even motivate them to learn more about mindfulness, meditation, and positive thinking in order to make these practices an important part of their lives as well.

In our final , we're going to talk about the importance of sleep in your life. As a final statement and tool for you to take away from this journey, I hope you will consider doing everything you can to make the process easier, which includes resting each night for an adequate amount of time. Getting a good night's rest may be the difference between success and failure because it has such a huge influence on how well the brain will function over the short and long-term. So, let's learn a little more about the importance of sleep and how it relates to the rhythms of our lives.

Chapter 13 Why Am I So Negative?

What is Negative Thinking?

It was already mentioned in the introduction but it bears repeating: negative thoughts are normal. We cannot escape the occasional low mood, worry, or gloomy thought. In fact, trying to ban all negativity from our lives just creates more negative stress because it puts unrealistic pressure on ourselves. It's perfectly natural to experience worry if you suddenly lose your job or to feel annoyed if your neighbors keep throwing loud parties late into the night. It's when you begin to fixate solely on these thoughts and feelings that they become a problem. In the context of this book, the phrase "negative thinking" doesn't refer to occasional passing thoughts or worry over one-off stressful situations, but rather to the habit of repetitive, persistent, pervasive negative thinking. This could come in the form of constantly replaying past events or conversations, overanalyzing, beating yourself up, fixating on a situation, or worrying obsessively about the future. People struggling with this habit might think negatively about themselves, others, or the world around them in general. Whatever form their negative thoughts take, however, eventually the habit will begin to seriously impact their lives.

Negative thinking can be sneaky as well. It can creep up on you without you really noticing it until suddenly, negative thoughts hold sway over your day or even your life. After all, no one sets out to develop a bad habit; it happens gradually over time and in subtle ways. We often get so caught up in our day-to-day lives that we rarely take the time to stop and really look at our thoughts. As a result, it is easy to engage in repetitive negative thinking without even realizing it. You might just notice that you're in a bad mood or that you feel "off" but upon closer examination, you realize that you've been mentally rehashing a recent fight with your mother all day. Learning to catch yourself as soon as you start to get caught up in a negative thought or story so that you can stop the momentum is just one of the strategies you'll learn in later .

There are a few types of negative thinking that commonly show up in people's lives, and they often overlap. These include: guilty thinking, "shoulding," all-or-nothing thinking, worst case scenario thinking, predicting the future, mind reading, blaming, comparing, and overall pessimism.

Guilty Thinking

When a person is caught up in guilty thinking, they often find themselves trapped in the past. They feel guilty for mistakes they have made, replaying them over and over again. Perhaps you said something in anger that hurt your spouse's feelings; while it's normal to feel remorse in this situation, a habitual negative thinker will continue to beat themselves up for their words and feel crippling guilt even after they've apologized to their spouse. Another common example is making a mistake at work. Perhaps you input an incorrect number on a report, resulting in embarrassment in front of your boss or in extra work needed from yourself or your colleagues to fix the error. We all make mistakes, but negative thinkers will be unable to let it go. They'll replay it over and over, beating themselves up and telling themselves things like, "I can't believe I didn't double-check those numbers. I'm such an idiot. I should never have volunteered to write that report. That meeting was so embarrassing, I looked like an incompetent screw-up. Heck, maybe I am!"

Guilty thinking often goes hand-in-hand with "shoulding" all-or-nothing thinking, and predicting the future.

Shoulding

This line of negative thinking happens when a person obsesses over what they "should" or "should not" do. In the example about the error at work, the person slipped into "should" thinking by telling themselves that they should have been more careful or that they should not have volunteered for the job. Perhaps you have been unhappy with your physical fitness and find yourself constantly thinking, "I shouldn't have eaten that. I should have gone to the gym today." While setting goals is admirable and important for our continued personal growth, constantly lecturing ourselves for things we have or have not done—or "shoulding on ourselves", in the words of motivational speaker Loretta Laroche (Laroche, 2008)—can be counterproductive to those goals. Instead of inspiring and motivating us, it just makes us feel worse about ourselves.

Should thinking often overlaps with guilty thinking, predicting the future, and mind reading.

All-or-Nothing Thinking

Always. Never. Every time. A person who finds themselves using words like these on a regular basis may be caught up in all-or-nothing thinking. If you are an all-or-nothing thinker, you see the world in black and white. Things are either good or bad. A certain aspect of your life always goes well or goes horribly. You are either perfect at something or a failure. So, how is this line of thinking negative? It leaves no room for normal human error or for happenstance. Say you are single and go out on a first date that doesn't go very well. If you are an all-or-nothing thinker, you might tell yourself, "I always screw up dating so why even bother trying? Relationships just never work out for me." Similarly, if you have a bad experience at a restaurant, you might think, "You can never find good customer service anymore. Society is just failing." This line of thinking ultimately lowers your level of regard for yourself and for the people around you.

All-or-nothing thinking often relates to worst case scenario thinking, predicting the future, and overall pessimism.

Worst Case Scenario Thinking/Worrying

Otherwise known as "catastrophizing" (Grohol, 2018), worst case scenario thinking or worrying happens when we believe in the worst possible outcome for a given situation. Recall our earlier example of an error at work. If you engage in worst case scenario thinking, you might worry and think, "I can't believe I made such a stupid mistake. I'm obviously going to get fired now." Perhaps you have a splitting headache and immediately think, "It must be a brain tumor." Similarly, perhaps a loved one is a bit late in contacting you and you start thinking, "There must have been a terrible accident." Clearly, such thinking can induce severe worry or even anxiety, particularly if it's a constant pattern.

Worst case scenario thinking often goes hand-in-hand with all-or-nothing thinking, predicting the future, and mind reading.

Predicting the Future

This line of negative thinking is very similar to worst case scenario thinking but it relates specifically to events and situations in the future. If you engage in this type of negative thinking, you view the potential for future happiness or success as very low. We could also call this "why bother" thinking. Imagine you line up an interview for your dream job; if you are caught in a pattern of predicting the future negatively, you might think, "I know I'm just going to be awkward and screw it up. Why should I even bother going?" Predicting-the-future thinking can influence your relationships as well. Perhaps you have moved to a new city and are invited to a party; your negative thought pattern might have you believe that people won't like you so you shouldn't attend.

Predicting the future thinking relates closely to worst case scenario thinking, all-or-nothing thinking, and overall pessimism. The future is always uncertain. Giving it certainty is only going to cause you mental anguish.

Mind Reading

When you engage in mind reading, you believe that you know what other people are thinking. You make assumptions about people's beliefs, thoughts, and feelings—and those assumptions are typically negative. You might walk by a group of co-workers and hear them laughing and think that they must be talking about you. If a friend doesn't respond to your text message immediately, you might jump to the conclusion that she must be angry with you. This line of thinking can be particularly harmful for your relationships because it makes you automatically assume the worst about people.

Mind reading often goes hand-in-hand with predicting the future and worst case scenario thinking.

Blaming

Blaming comes in two varieties: self-blame and blame of others. People who self-blame feel that they are responsible for everything that goes wrong in their lives. From their company not landing a prospective client to a special dinner not turning out well to missing an appointment because of traffic, they will believe that it was all their fault. Holding yourself accountable and taking responsibility for your actions and behaviors is healthy, but self-blame takes this to an unhealthy level, leading to low self-esteem and feelings of failure. When people perpetually place the blame on others, on the other hand, they abdicate their responsibility for any role they might have played. Someone who blames others might complain about their overly chatty coworker who prevents them from getting their work done rather than taking responsibility for their own lack of productivity.

Similarly, they might choose to complain daily about how other drivers make their commute so long rather than just accepting the reality that everyone is sitting in the same traffic. Blaming can negatively impact your relationships, as well as diminish your sense of control over your own life and your ability to accept life as it is.

Blaming goes hand-in-hand with all-or-nothing thinking and pessimism.

Comparing

Comparing ourselves to others and finding ourselves lacking is a very common form of negative thinking. Virtually everyone has experienced instances when their inner critic has piped up. People might compare their looks, their relationship status, their wealth, their career path, or their material belongings. They also might compare themselves to their friends and family or to complete strangers. Constant comparison can lead to an overall feeling of dissatisfaction with your life and lowered self-esteem.

Comparing often goes along with worst case scenario thinking and predicting the future.

Pessimism

This is too good to last. Life is just supposed to be hard. People can't be trusted. Nothing is certain but death and taxes. If you find yourself making statements like these often, you might be engaging in overall pessimistic thinking. When you have this mindset, you expect things to go poorly. You expect other people and yourself to let you down. You find it hard to accept or trust when good things happen. Some people who are deeply caught in pessimistic thinking can even begin to take pleasure in situations going awry because it validates their worldview.

Pessimism relates closely to worst case scenario thinking, predicting the future, and blaming.

What Causes Negative Thinking?

Have you ever wondered, "Why am I so negative?" Or perhaps a loved one has told you, "You need to look on the bright side more often." Where does negative thinking stem from? Why do some people look at life as a glass half full while others see it as half empty? Is it nature or nurture?

It's become a commonly accepted idea that we are born with our own natural happiness set point. This is the level of happiness that we experience regardless of what is happening in our lives; whether everything is going well or we are experiencing challenges, our happiness set point remains generally the same. In fact, it's been shown that even when people experience a significant positive event like winning the lottery or a significant negative event like a serious medical diagnosis, their happiness set point returns to its baseline after about a year (Bloom, 2017). If people have happiness set points, it stands to reason that we also have our own individual levels of positivity and negativity. So, it may be the case that some people are just more predisposed to negative thinking than others. This is the nature side of the coin.

Our early childhood experiences also impact our personalities, mindsets, and worldviews. If you were raised in a household where negative thinking was prevalent, you likely learned some of the same behaviors. Perhaps you had an overly critical parent, causing you to compare and judge yourself harshly later in life. A parent who frequently expressed pessimistic thoughts may have taught you that the world is harsh or that the cards are stacked against you. More traumatic childhood experiences, such as neglect or abandonment, can lead to negative thinking patterns as well. Someone who suffered early trauma may engage in worst case scenario thinking, finding it hard to trust other people or take their word. Clearly, nurture plays as large a part as nature in determining whether you will be plagued by negative thinking.

A pattern of negative thinking can also be caused by stressful life events beyond childhood. The end of a relationship, the loss of a job, or a health scare can all spark negative thoughts which if not addressed can soon spiral out of control into habitual pessimistic thinking. Negative thinking functions like a feedback loop: the more we focus our attention on what's going wrong in our lives or in the world, the worse we feel. And the worse we feel, the harder it will be to have a positive attitude. It becomes a vicious cycle and those grooves of negativity in our mental track just get deeper and deeper.

For some people, negative thinking can even develop into an addiction. People for whom negativity becomes an addiction derive a sort of pleasure from the habit. As mentioned earlier, pessimistic thoughts can be used as a way to validate a person's worldview. Similarly, negative thoughts can be used to cement a person's identity ("I'm always a victim") or to try to make sense of or control the world around them ("People are just bad, that's all there is to it.") (Colier, 2019).

So much for how the habit of negative thinking can develop. Where do the specific negative thoughts themselves come from? If you begin to pay attention to the content of your negative thoughts, you'll notice that they fall into one of two camps: anxiety or fear about the future or guilt or anger about the past. We all experience these feelings from time to time, but habitual negative thinkers dwell on the past or the future and find it hard or even impossible to let their thoughts go and focus on the present.

For many people, negative thinking crops up in specific situations or with specific people. You may experience negative thinking in the form of social anxiety. Perhaps you worry that people won't like you or are talking about you behind your back in social settings; you might also find yourself constantly comparing yourself to others or judging them harshly. Some people are plagued by negative thinking in their work environments; they might complain constantly about their boss, their coworkers, or their customers, or demand perfection from themselves and others. Negativity can crop up at home as well. Perhaps you find yourself constantly criticizing your family members; you might also be consumed with worry about the health and well-being of your family or feel like you need to "do it all" yourself and thus make yourself a martyr. Your negativity could center on your body image and looks, your finances, or politics and the general state of the world.

What Are the Effects of Negative Thinking?

Breaking a habit like negative thinking is hard, but truly comprehending the impact of habitual negative thinking can give you the motivation to make a change. You might not even realize all the ways in which constant negative thoughts are intruding on your life.

One major effect is fairly obvious right off the bat: negative thinking creates negative feelings. People who constantly think gloomy thoughts will often feel irritable, sad, angry, hopeless, anxious, or apathetic. Habitual negative thinking can even develop into a more serious mental health condition such as depression or anxiety disorder. The bottom line is that thinking gloomy thoughts makes you feel bad.

Constant negativity can take a toll on your physical health as well. For example, constant worrying can disrupt your sleep and keep you up at night, leaving you feeling drained of energy and unable to concentrate. When you are tired and lethargic, you might be less likely to exercise or make healthy food choices. The stress produced by constant negative thinking can also drive people to unhealthy coping mechanisms such as smoking cigarettes or drinking alcohol in excess. And the list of physical effects doesn't end there. Perpetual anxiety or anger can increase your blood pressure and impact your digestion. Constant stress, such as that brought on by worry and negativity, raises the levels of cortisol produced in the body; this in turn can lower your immune system's ability to fight off infections. Studies have even found that pessimism, cynicism, and depression can increase a person's chances of heart disease and stroke (Hoffman, 2015).

In addition to eroding both your mental and your physical health, perpetual negative thinking affects your life in many other ways as well. While it might not seem obvious, one area of your life that can be impacted by negative thinking is your finances. The feelings of sadness, hopelessness, or depression brought on by negative thinking might make it hard for you to focus at work, thus reducing your productivity and eventually even threatening your job security. Similarly, negative self-judgments could keep you stuck in menial or low-paying work and make you less likely to apply for more lucrative employment opportunities. Some people turn to shopping as a way to distract themselves from negative thoughts and make themselves feel better; this can lead to overspending or even a shopping addiction.

Over time, negative thinking patterns can damage relationships as well. Most people won't want to spend time with someone who constantly complains, criticizes, or belittles others. In fact, research suggests that just listening to another person complaining can actually have negative health impacts; the brain of the person listening releases stress hormones that can reduce cognitive functions and lead to overall greater levels of stress (Montenegro, 2015). If you are a perpetual negative thinker, you may find friends or romantic partners begin to pull away from you. Similarly, you might have trouble making new friends. Work relationships can also be challenged by constant negativity; your colleagues may be hesitant to involve you in group work or to help you out with a project. Being labeled as difficult at work can even threaten your job itself.

A negative mindset can prevent you from solving problems effectively. This might sound counterintuitive: after all, shouldn't thinking about your problems help you find solutions? The truth is, overanalyzing and ruminating on negative events or situations can lead to analysis paralysis, preventing you from ever taking any action at all to address your problems. Habitual negative thinkers tend to be close-minded as well, impeding their ability to think outside the box and see creative solutions. They also might be less likely to reach out to others for help or advice.

Finally, negativity begets more negativity. Remember the feedback loop mentioned earlier? You might have noticed how on days when you wake up on the wrong side of the bed, everything else seems to go wrong, too. You spill coffee on your favorite shirt. You stub your toe. You miss your bus and end up being late for work. Some people believe that you attract negative events and situations by putting out negative energy. However, it could just be that when you are focusing on the negative, that is what you will see. What we place our attention on grows. If you constantly fixate on what is going wrong in your life, you will be more likely to notice every little bad thing and less likely to notice the good things.

How Can I Silence Those Negative Thoughts?

In later , we'll discuss specific strategies and practices to help you tame that negative voice in your head. For now, though, simply focus on becoming aware of your negative thoughts. Take some time to examine what forms they typically take. Understanding the causes of your negative thinking can be an important first step in breaking the habit. We cannot change what we're not aware of.

For example, when you determine what type of negative thinker you are—worst case scenario thinker, blamer, all-or-nothing thinker—you'll begin to notice those thoughts more often as they crop up, providing the opportunity to consciously let them go. Similarly, if you realize you tend to think more negatively in certain situations (at work, with your spouse, etc.), you can begin to think of ways to shift those situations so that you can feel more positive about them. The more you understand your negative thinking patterns, the better prepared you will be to choose the right strategies and practices to help you change them.

You may want to keep a journal or take notes on your smartphone for a few days to help you track your thinking patterns. When you notice yourself caught in a negativity loop, take a moment to jot down some of the details about it. Where were you when the negative thoughts popped up? Who were you with and what were you doing? What form did your negative thoughts take? Were you focused on the past or the future? Did the negativity center on yourself or on external factors (other people, world events, etc.)? How do the negative thoughts make you feel emotionally and physically? Do you notice any tension, tightness, or clenching in your body?

Becoming more aware of your negative thoughts can be uncomfortable. For example, you may begin to see clearly how your negativity has hurt those around you. It can be unpleasant to realize that your behavior has been harmful but such a realization is the only way to make amends and move forward with new behaviors. Awareness is a necessary first step. Your habit of negative thinking did not develop overnight, so breaking the habit will not happen immediately either. In order to truly break the pattern and clear mental space for new habits, you need to be willing to examine your thoughts and work through any uncomfortable emotions or knowledge they may bring up.

Think of your negative thought pattern as a physical illness. In order to know how best to treat you, your doctor would first need to perform tests to determine what type of illness you had and where it stemmed from. Having a clear understanding of the causes and effects of your negative thinking (the source of the infection and the symptoms) will set you up to "treat" it more effectively using the tips and strategies found in the following .

Conclusion

Optimism is not just a state of the mind; it is also shown through your actions and words. If your work gets canceled due to inclement weather, an optimistic person would enjoy the time off or work on something else to be productive. Whereas positivity is about having a positive attitude - even when challenging situations arise. One psychologist once theorized that you attract what you think about most. This is the Law of Attraction and it says that when you think of and focus on something, it will happen. Remember how you wished to not see a certain person and you did? You focused your thoughts and energy on that particular person, and there they were! Well, that's law of attraction.

This theory is true whether you are thinking negative or positive thoughts. The more you think of negative thoughts, the more you'll encounter negative things. Let's look at this scenario. Imagine you're in a taxi hurrying your way to work with a traffic jam on the street. Human nature tells you to start worrying because you might be late to work. When you do, you decide to get out of the cab and power-walk your way through the traffic jam. As you are walking, you keep looking at your watch, ticking and ticking. Twenty minutes until work became ten that rapidly became five. At this point you're stressed and sending out all types of negative energy. As you cross the street while looking at your watch, a car hits you. It may not be a big hit but you still felt the pain. And because you are very anxious and stressed during that time, you shout at the driver and confront him. Now the clock says you are late. With this scenario, you can see that a cascade of events will happen once you strongly think negative thoughts.

The same is true when you think of more positive thoughts. When you are about to enter your workplace, you started telling yourself that you can do all your tasks for the day. You greeted everyone with a smile on your face, found your way to your desk and pleasantly started working. Even if a pile of unfinished papers greeted you that morning, you did not panic. Instead, you took a look at each of them and prioritized them. You grouped all papers needing immediate attention and you did the same for the not-so-urgent ones. With a positive attitude, you gradually finish them all without undue stress.

Adopting positivity, just like other processes, takes time. You need to consciously make an effort to practice it every moment of every day, whatever comes your way, until it becomes a good habit. Again, it is believed that it takes 30-days of consistently doing something to form a habit. Adopting positivity is a commitment and you have to be faithful in adopting positivity not only in your thoughts, but also in your actions and words. Below are some strategies to begin with positivity.

Be healthy

Many people don't think they can manage their problems because they are sick or because they feel too weak to accomplish their tasks. If this is the case, the best way to counteract it is to stay healthy. Start a healthy lifestyle by eating a balanced and healthy diet – one that has the right amount of carbohydrates, proteins, and other sources that is right for you. A food regimen that contains plenty of vegetables and fruits is good because they contain vitamins and minerals that are essential for the proper functioning of your cells.

Exercise is another way of maintaining a healthy lifestyle. Exercise does not only make your body stronger and your muscles larger, but exercise is a good way of relieving stress and energizing yourself. If you exercise regularly, you'll have the zest to work the whole day. Without exercise or good nutrition, you'll often feel lazy, inadequate and weak.

Change the way you think

Though changing the way you think is as difficult as changing the way you were brought up, it is something that you can achieve over time. Emotions are things that we ultimately have control over, and we have the ability to change the way we feel about certain things. Much of it can be changed shift of perspectives or the way we view certain situations. Think of ways to turn your negative thoughts into positive ones and do not let these negative thoughts control you. Ask yourself, what is one positive thing I can take out of this negative perspective? Then, look for another positive thing, and focus your energy on those positive things instead of the negative ones.

Start positive self- talk

You don't need other people to encourage you. You can do it to yourself. A simple "Good job!" or "Congratulations!" can already do the trick. What is even better with this method is that you don't need a specific time to do it. You can do this when you are busy, or when you are not doing anything, or when you are eating. You don't need anyone to do this, either. It may sound silly but it works. Talk to yourself like talking to a friend; encourage yourself, praise yourself and always remind yourself that you are powerful enough to overcome all the challenges that you will encounter in the future.

If you are doing something for the first time, don't be afraid. A negative self-talk may sound like, "I don't know how to do this," but a positive self-talk would say, "This is a new experience and I will learn new things from this." If you want to do something but you don't have the resources, a negative self-talk would say, "I cannot do it because I need this first." A positive self-talk would most likely be, "I can do it. I just need to get this first."

Always look forward to something

Every day, you get to encounter different challenges, experience various events or meet new people. When you see the things happening to you as being part of something great, then you are attracting positive things into your life.

Positivity and optimism start with a positive attitude. You can gain optimism by anticipating that something good will come out of whatever it is you are going through right now.